ENTERPRISE BUSINESS ARCHITECTURE

*The Formal Link
between
Strategy and Results*

OTHER AUERBACH PUBLICATIONS

The ABCs of IP Addressing
Gilbert Held
ISBN: 0-8493-1144-6

The ABCs of LDAP: How to Install, Run, and Administer LDAP Services
Reinhard Voglmaier
ISBN: 0-8493-1346-5

The ABCs of TCP/IP
Gilbert Held
ISBN: 0-8493-1463-1

Building a Wireless Office
Gilbert Held
ISBN: 0-8493-1271-X

The Complete Project Management Office Handbook
Gerald M. Hill
ISBN: 0-8493-2173-5

Enhancing LAN Performance, 4th Edition
Gilbert Held
ISBN: 0-8493-1942-0

Information Security Management Handbook, 5th Edition
Harold F. Tipton and Micki Krause, Editors
ISBN: 0-8493-1997-8

Information Security Policies and Procedures: A Practitioner's Reference 2nd Edition
Thomas R. Peltier
ISBN: 0-8493-1958-7

Information Security Policies, Procedures, and Standards: Guidelines for Effective Information Security Management
Thomas R. Peltier
ISBN: 0-8493-1137-3

Information Security Risk Analysis
Thomas R. Peltier
ISBN: 0-8493-0880-1

Information Technology for Manufacturing: Reducing Costs and Expanding Capabilities
Kevin Aki, John Clemons, and Mark Cubine
ISBN: 1-57444-359-3

Interpreting the CMMI: A Process Improvement Approach
Margaret Kulpa and Kurt Johnson
ISBN: 0-8493-1654-5

IS Management Handbook, 8th Edition
Carol V. Brown and Heikki Topi
ISBN: 0-8493-1595-6

ISO 9000:2000 for Software and Systems Providers
Robert Bamford and William Deibler, III
ISBN: 0-8493-2063-1

Managing a Network Vulnerability Assessment
Thomas R. Peltier and Justin Peltier
ISBN: 0-8493-1270-1

A Practical Approach to WBEM/CIM Management
Chris Hobbs
ISBN: 0-8493-2306-1

A Practical Guide to Security Engineering and Information Assurance
Debra Herrmann
ISBN: 0-8493-1163-2

Practical Network Design Techniques, 2nd Edition: A Complete Guide for WANs and LANs
Gilbert Held and S. Ravi Jagannathan
ISBN: 0-8493-2019-4

Real Process Improvement Using the CMMI
Michael West
ISBN: 0-8493-2109-3

Six Sigma Software Development
Christine B. Tayntor
ISBN: 0-8493-1193-4

Software Architecture Design Patterns in Java
Partha Kuchana
ISBN: 0-8493-2142-5

Software Configuration Management
Jessica Keyes
ISBN: 0-8493-1976-5

A Technical Guide to IPSec Virtual Private Networks
James S. Tiller
ISBN: 0-8493-0876-3

Telecommunications Cost Management
Brian DiMarsico, Thomas Phelps IV, and William A. Yarberry, Jr.
ISBN: 0-8493-1101-2

AUERBACH PUBLICATIONS

www.auerbach-publications.com
To Order Call: 1-800-272-7737 • Fax: 1-800-374-3401
E-mail: orders@crcpress.com

ENTERPRISE
BUSINESS
ARCHITECTURE

The Formal Link between Strategy and Results

Ralph Whittle and Conrad B. Myrick

AUERBACH PUBLICATIONS

A CRC Press Company
Boca Raton   London   New York   Washington, D.C.

Library of Congress Cataloging-in-Publication Data

Whittle, Ralph.
    Enterprise business architecture : the formal link between strategy and results / Ralph Whittle, Conrad B. Myrick.
       p. cm.
    Includes bibliographical references and index.
    ISBN 0-8493-2788-1 (alk. paper)
    1. Organizational effectiveness. 2. Strategic planning. I. Myrick, Conrad B. II. Title.

    HD58.9W53 2004
    658.4′02--dc22

                                             2004047464

Visit the Auerbach Web site at www.auerbach-publications.com

© 2005 by CRC Press LLC
Auerbach is an imprint of CRC Press LLC

No claim to original U.S. Government works
International Standard Book Number 0-8493-2788-1
Library of Congress Card Number 2004047464
Printed in the United States of America 1 2 3 4 5 6 7 8 9 0

DEDICATION

To Mom and Dad from a grateful son. My sincere thanks for your
guidance during my formative years, for your influence on my values
and beliefs, and for your encouragement throughout my life.

R.W.

To those who insist the world is flat: "...here be Dragons".
To those who thought I could not: they drove me to prove them wrong.
To my wife, Dona, who said I could: that was what encouraged
me to reveal the world is round.

C.B.M.

CONTENTS

LIST OF FIGURES

LIST OF TABLES

PREFACE

Almost every enterprise today lacks a formal architecture, similar in concept to the blueprint of a house or office building. No one will ever consider building a complex structure such as a skyscraper, automobile, ship, or airplane without blueprints based on a complete set of integrated architectures. However, we consistently build, merge, reorganize, and run enterprises without a set of equivalent blueprints or architectures. When investigating problems in this environment, it usually boils down to the fact that something was overlooked, a connection was forgotten, or a relationship was missed.

These blueprints and architectures form the nexus between all components, parts, and pieces, and create a whole, complete entity. The typical deliverables from a corporate strategy usually include "something that you have to build, the what" and "something you have to achieve, the result" to provide a new or enhanced operational capability. This "something that you have to build" is more precisely defined in an architecture or a modification to existing architectures. We often represent the architecture in a formal model illustrating all of the components and their connections. As for the "something you have to achieve," you have to implement the supporting corporate initiatives to produce the desired results predicted and expected in the strategy.

Some companies have developed extended enterprises,[1] set up virtual enterprises,[2] and designed business webs[3] or value nets[4] all without a formal architecture of the business. Consequently, most executives feel that these formalities are not necessary or they are unaware that a formal enterprise business architecture approach exists. Eventually, they get a new endeavor up and running, not realizing the missed business efficiencies, opportunities of "speed to market," and cost savings. Additionally, they discover that this new endeavor is hard to sustain and maintain; but that is the status quo from their perspective. Failing to understand the value of a formal architectural approach, many say, "That's just the way it is." But it does not have to be that way.

Architectures are critical in the construction industry for building structures and for maintaining them for years to come. The architecture is the formal link between the home owners' dreams and the reality of their new home. For example, would you ever allow the building of your dream home by a company that did not draw up a set of blueprints for you to review? Would you ever allow the major addition to your existing home of a sunroom, patio, and pool with supporting landscapes without analyzing the blueprints? No one is willing to let a truck back up to an empty lot and off-load the carpenters, bricklayers, plumbers, electricians, and heating and cooling personnel and let them start building the house without a blueprint. However, we somehow think this approach is OK when building or maintaining a business enterprise. How do you think the CEO, COO, CFO, and CIO feel when presented with a major corporate strategic initiative without any supporting enterprise blueprints? Do you not think that they intuitively feel there is a need for understanding enterprise business, organizational, and infrastructure linkages in order to make sound decisions on initiatives and priorities but are seldom presented with any formal proof of such?

Consider this: We consistently build and rebuild enterprises with inherent architectural design flaws, which create enormous inefficiencies and missed opportunities and cause havoc within the enterprise. The proof of this is found in the frequent corporate reorganizations, layoffs, failed corporate initiatives, project cost overruns, and numerous business unit failures. In almost every case the current enterprise linkages are not formally documented, well articulated, sufficiently detailed, well engineered, tightly integrated, or adaptive enough to respond to ever-changing market forces and opportunities. Why? For one reason: There is no published literature or approach today that presents a formal, deliberate, and demonstrable method that systematically addresses this problem or offers a successfully field-tested technique and guide on how to go about satisfying this need. Do not be deceived; most of the literature that claims to address enterprise architecture approaches does so only as an aside and is usually so noninclusive of all of the other enterprise architectures that it only corroborates that it is a purely academic exercise.

One of the keys to successful strategic planning and business engineering is an integrated enterprise architecture approach. This book is about understanding and building formal, but practical, industrial-strength, integrated enterprise architectures starting with the enterprise business architecture. Once this architecture is developed, understood, and implemented, the enterprise can avoid the previously mentioned missed opportunities and pre- and postimplementation inefficiencies. Every individual, team, department, organization, and business unit will have an understanding of the entire enterprise, not just its functional domain or area. When considering new business opportunities, evaluating strategic initiatives, and implementing new technology capabilities, the decision makers will have a far better understanding of the impact on the whole enterprise. The net of it is better predictable results and results aligned with the vision and objectives of the integrated enterprise. This ultimately translates into higher profits and a competitive advantage for the stakeholders.

To integrate and empirically derive all of the enterprise architectures, we need one base or foundational architecture, a central plexus between the strategy, its supporting architectures, and the predictable results of the planned initiatives. This architecture must be the superstructure that sits on top of all other enterprise architectures and is their hierarchical parent. Consequently, any change at the top must necessarily propagate down through the other architectures; otherwise, the integration is compromised. This hierarchical parent is the enterprise business architecture (EBA).

Therefore, the primary focus of this book is the EBA, and the approaches and techniques necessary for allowing rigorous integration with other architectures, initiatives, and strategies. The other supporting and enabling enterprise architectures, the technology (including data/information, application, and network/technology), security, and organizational architectures, are addressed individually and collectively, and in great detail in numerous other books and publications. The same is true for the multitude of books and publications on business and information technology (IT) strategy. This book will therefore not focus in detail on these topics, but they will be referenced in connection with the integration and creation of the EBA.

When you truly have a holistic architectural approach, it is somewhat difficult to completely isolate for review and analysis an integrated component, such as the EBA, from other architectures. Therefore, at times the reader may think this text is about developing strategy or IT architectures. It may seem so because tightly integrated components and parts cannot be fully examined without a clear reference and understanding of the entity as a whole and without considering all of the relationships between components, both business and IT, and the supporting corporate strategies. This is the same characteristic found in well-integrated enterprises. That is to say, any serious analysis of the enterprise cannot simply focus on one isolated functional area, but it must expand the focus to understand the impact on the whole enterprise and its external and internal relationships as well.

The formalities associated with building an enterprise business architecture and integrating it with enabling and supporting technologies do not require you to discard your current strategic planning methodologies.

The EBA does not require you to toss out all of your business process analysis and reengineering tools, techniques, methods, and software development methodologies. The EBA is, however, a disciplined and rigorous expansion in the area of architecture development used in most of these methodologies. It is another tool for understanding the enterprise, analyzing its opportunities, developing initiatives to sustain a competitive advantage, and bridging the gap to IT. The intent is to use the formal enterprise business architecture as a complement to other approaches and methodologies.

In some cases, when starting to build the EBA, you may prefer to start with a division, region, or some other enterprise component. This is acceptable as long as you consider the component a self-contained business unit or entity, always keeping in mind that it is part of a greater whole, and not some arbitrary grouping of organizational departments. For example, you may have one business unit with a pure product focus and another business unit with a pure service focus, with the two seemingly not related. This might have occurred as the result of a merger or acquisition. Just keep in mind the point about the self-contained business unit and stay away from some sort of gerrymandered organizational entity.

We believe that this approach will provide keen insight into your strategic thinking. Adopting formal integrated enterprise architectures and building the EBA does not really require several new skills, but it does require a realistic and practiced discipline and rigor. It is more about behavior than just learning a new skill. It requires inspirational leadership with an extensive amount of collaboration between various team members. It also requires a dedicated customer-centric focus from the whole enterprise, not just a single organization or division.

REFERENCES

1. Francois B. Vernadat, *Enterprise Modeling and Integration: Principles and Applications* (New York: Chapman & Hall, 1996), 4.
2. Patrick McHugh, Giorgio Merli, and William A. Wheeler III, *Beyond Business Process Reengineering: Towards the Holonic Enterprise* (New York: John Wiley & Sons, Inc., 1995), 4.
3. Don Tapscott, David Ticoll, and Alex Lowy, *Digital Capital: Harnessing the Power of Business Webs* (Cambridge, MA: Harvard Business School Press, 2000), 4.
4. David Bovet and Joseph Martha, *Value Nets: Breaking the Supply Chain to Unlock Hidden Profits* (New York: John Wiley & Sons, Inc., 2000), 2.

ABOUT THE AUTHORS

Ralph Whittle is a Strategic Business/IT Consultant and subject matter expert in Enterprise Business Architecture development and implementation. He has built Enterprise Business Architectures in various industries, such as manufacturing, healthcare, finance, and technology. He has worked in the IT industry for over 26 years, conducting engagements in enterprise business process modeling, strategic/tactical business planning, enterprise business requirements analysis, enterprise business architecture and IT architecture integration, strategic frameworks integration with systems development methodologies and IT service offering enhancement. He is a co-author of a patent (currently pending) for a Strategic Business/IT Planning framework.

Conrad B. Myrick has over 27 years of Information Technology (IT) background, including software and systems design, development, implementation, central and account support, systems programming, data center operations, and 6 years of Strategic IT Planning consulting and management.

Conrad has led Strategic IT Planning/ Enterprise Architecture definition projects for commercial clients in multiple countries and industries (Fortune 500 to start-up). He is an expert in determining client requirements, engagement management, and execution in the development of enterprise-wide strategic IT plans providing business and technology alignment. He is experienced in creating the enterprise architecture models and transition plans which integrate people, processes, and technology, and direct the strategic and tactical implementation of various IT solutions.

Conrad also provided the genesis and fostered the evolution of a strategic IT planning approach, processes, and techniques spanning the IT services continuum. He co-authored the patent (currently pending) and led the research and development effort for a comprehensive Strategic Business/IT Planning framework. Deployment of this framework in a leading IT services company greatly improved delivery consistency and reliability of those services, and enhanced the internal and client understanding and adoption of the strategic IT planning process.

ACKNOWLEDGMENTS

We acknowledge other consultants and authors for their insight and leadership. In many cases, we chose to use existing terms already defined by these authors, rather than inventing new buzzwords. Neal Goldstein, an excellent consultant and mentor, motivated us to pursue architectural and integration concepts. Steven H. Spewak and Steven C. Hill, who wrote *Enterprise Architecture Planning: Developing a Blueprint for Data, Applications and Technology*, provided us with a foundation for integrating the enterprise business architecture. As for books with similar strategic themes, ours extends their concepts with a formal, disciplined, and practical business engineering approach. You might consider *The Great Transition* by James Martin, *Digital Capital* by Don Tapscott et al., and *The Fifth Discipline* by Peter Senge. Our approach uses James Martin's "value streams" to build out and integrate Don Tapscott et al.'s "value maps" using Peter Senge's "systems thinking." These consultants and authors specifically, and many others were a constant source of inspiration.

We also acknowledge the team at CRC Press. Many thanks to our publisher Rich O'Hanley, for believing in our dream, and to Andrea Demby and Claire Miller for transforming our dream into the pages of a real book.

Our web site seemed never to get off the drawing board until Phil Breden took over responsibility for its development. He made it easy for us, so we just followed his advice and recommendations. We are most thankful for his support.

INTRODUCTION

OVERVIEW

Almost every enterprise today lacks a formal business architecture, similar in concept to the blueprint of a house or office building. These architectures and blueprints are critical in developing and maintaining complex business enterprises because one of the keys to successful strategic planning and engineering is an integrated enterprise architecture approach. It all begins with the **enterprise business architecture (EBA)** and its component linkages. This book is about an approach to building a formal, but practical, industrial-strength EBA.

Part I introduces some of the terms and concepts supporting the EBA. The importance of architectures is highlighted and you are challenged to research and analyze the available architectures in your own enterprise. If you believe the architectures are important and necessary, then ask yourself what problems and needs have you identified in your research and analysis. You will find some of the same problems and needs chronicled in this book. Through your assessment, it is to be expected that you will not only understand the recommended EBA solution, but also appreciate the new behavior, rigor, and discipline required to harness its potential.

Part II illustrates a high-level approach for building the enterprise business architecture. This portion of the book will provide you with examples, insight, and guidance for determining the value of this approach for your enterprise, but it is not intended for use as a user's manual or "cookbook." As you will see, architecture development and modeling skills are easy to learn; however, the supporting rigor, discipline, structure, and practice required in the new behavior are the challenges and are not normally found in any manual.

Part III provides some suggestions, recommendations, and ideas for implementing the formal EBA approach to architectures, models, and frameworks. This part is based on experiences gained from a number of successful engagements and projects. The reader should expect to have and see the "proof of the pudding" in understanding the evolutionary nature of the implementation of the approach. As you will see, this is not a one-time slam-dunk project, but a new corporate behavior and discipline.

In developing the approach there is a focus on several underlying themes that complement understanding of the method:

- *Viewing the enterprise holistically through the eyes of the customer* and not from some political or organizational view
- *Engineering the enterprise* by integrating and connecting all the necessary components, but not sawing pieces apart and slamming others together
- *Developing component architectures* through a formal process decomposition
- *Improving communications* among all teams, departments, organizations, regions, divisions, and business units throughout the enterprise
- *Accepting the evolution of architecture development* rather than waiting ages for the improbable architectural births in a fully grown state
- *Transitioning to graphical-based thinking* from text-based thinking
- *Using strategic business thinking to drive* the building of enabling infrastructure technologies — strategy to results
- *Determining a well-informed and appropriate course of action* by providing pragmatic information to the reader

I

UNDERSTANDING
THE APPROACH

1

INTRODUCTION

It was the best of times; it was the worst of times ...

—**Charles Dickens,**
A Tale of Two Cities

In every economic cycle, some industries experience the best of times in terms of growth, revenue, and profit, while others experience the worst of times with serious downturns in these same areas. A few years later the roles reverse for some, and for others, things just continually get worse and worse. Just look at the turnover in the Fortune 500 list. We marvel at the success of some enterprises and are troubled at the failures of others.

Most struggling enterprises blame the economy, the current administration in Washington, political uncertainty in other parts of the world, and many other external factors. Even those enterprises that are doing well may cast blame in similar directions, implying higher levels of growth and profit were missed due to these external factors. Corporate greed and executive malfeasance are also high on the list as well.

It seems that the typical enterprise is always overwhelmed and chaotic, even in the best of times. Many corporate outcomes are not predictable, but are merely hoped for expectations. Mergers and acquisitions breed havoc on the surviving entities, and products rushed to market fail to meet quality standards and consumer needs. Then downsizing ultimately sends talented people to the unemployment line. With all of this uncertainty and confusion, investors bail out and things continue to go downhill from there.

There is another point of view. The enterprise is not about chaos; it is about connectivity and causality and understanding those relationships to both internal and external factors. This connectivity, causality, and understanding are found in an architecture of the business, a unifying structure that enables the execution of the strategy through its initiatives to achieve results. Without knowing this, it is fair to perceive the enterprise as chaotic and unpredictable, but it is our own responsibility to solve these problems and stop blaming the economy or some other external factors. We have to fess up to this responsibility and stop acting like a spectator at a sporting event just cheering for the home team. We have to get down into the arena and commit to a long-term solution. We have to suppress the quick-fix mentality, view the enterprise holistically, and develop insightful solutions that are responsive to customer demands and adaptive to the changing business climate.

However, there is a conundrum. We know that no matter how many poorly planned projects we inflict on the enterprise, in most cases, it somehow seems to eventually return to a state of equilibrium in spite of the upheaval and pandemonium the projects create. Somehow, it seems to organically heal the self-inflicted wounds and recover. But why do we always leave stability to serendipity? Why do we not just skip the upheaval and pandemonium and begin with a reasonable state of equilibrium? We usually cannot because most of these poorly planned projects are implemented independently and most implementers are unaware of the enterprise linkages that they are violating, fracturing, or ignoring. Instead of thrashing around in this environment of turmoil, we need to boldly stand on the threshold of a new era of structure and order, and take the steps to embrace it.

The building blocks of order and structure lie in the framework that defines the engineered integration of enterprise architectures. This framework is comprised of blueprints and architectures that create the formal links between all component parts and pieces and create a complete and harmonious entity. To integrate and empirically derive all enterprise architectures, we need one base or foundational architecture, a central plexus between the strategy, its supporting architectures, and the predicable results of its planned initiatives. This architecture must be the superstructure that sits on top of all other enterprise architectures and is their hierarchical parent. Consequently, any change at the top must propagate down through the other architectures; otherwise, the integration is compromised. This hierarchical parent is the **enterprise business architecture (EBA)** with all its component linkages.

The **EBA formal links** are defined as the fundamental and essential links that unite the enterprise to form a harmonious whole. These relationships are further defined in formal and disciplined terms. Henceforth, these links are characterized in architectures representing the business as a manifestation of the corporate strategy, achieving the results delivered by the enterprise initiatives. Please refer to Figure 1.1.

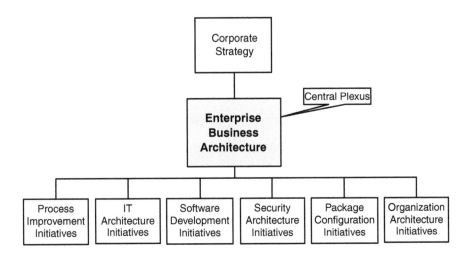

Figure 1.1 The EBA Formal Links

Today we operate in an environment more technically complex than at any other time, and it is getting more complicated every day. At times we feel out of control, awash in the daily chaos of quick fixes to problems that eventually degrade process efficiency, cloud initiative effectiveness, affect product quality, render poor customer service, and ultimately wipe out profits. There are no quick fixes for these faltering enterprises. If there were, we would have already implemented them.

The quick-fix mentality is symptomatic of bigger problems caused by poor designs, inherent design flaws, fractured architectures, weak integrations, and an inherently poor understanding of the EBA formal links. We need the long-term view, a permanent fix, and an adaptive design that is fully integrated. To get in control, you must design control into the enterprise and not let it suffer the consequences of unaligned functional management. Either you control the enterprise as a natural extension of your vision and strategy or the enterprise controls you through unpredictable chaotic events.

There are no guarantees of success or hyped-up promises of glory. Only a choice between staying put in an unstructured, chaotic, inherently flawed system or engineering your way out of this mess with the EBA. It is a tough decision, one made only by visionary leaders with a commitment to creating their view of the future and understanding the opportunities for success.

WHY IS THE EBA SO IMPORTANT OR EVEN NECESSARY?

As the 21st century begins, we find ourselves entering not only a new century, but also a new era. New and different ways of doing business are revolutionizing our industries, commerce, and governments. The convergence of communications and computing across the Internet, wireless technology, and abundant bandwidth are fueling this revolution. These unparalleled events are occurring throughout the world in every industry segment from the small family-size businesses all the way up to the largest corporations in the world.

Phenomenal opportunities are available to those who can take a vision and, through creativity and innovation, develop that vision into the next megaenterprise. What is enabling this revolution, providing its momentum, and sustaining its rapid progress? If we were in real estate, we might say it is three things: location, location, location. However, in this new era, fundamentally it is *architecture, architecture, architecture*. The architectural approaches and concepts are evolving for enterprises, but at different paces.

- *Architectures in the dark* — In this evolutionary state there are no real approaches, rules, or standards. Whatever exists is unknown, undefined, and not understood.
- *Architectures by chance* — In this state, the architectures are beginning to evolve, but any connectivity between disparate entities is coincidental.
- *Architectures by default* — In this state, the architectures are defined and managed by the hardware vendors, software package vendors, or next "hot" project that is going to save the enterprise.
- *Architectures by design* — This is the preferred state of evolutionary development. The architectures of the enterprise are designed, engineered, maintained, and adaptive to the external environment.

Those enterprises adopting the new rules of the 21st century and developing into the next group of megaenterprises have or are building integrated and adaptive architectures that enable these visions. It is a new enterprise — an enterprise that is designed and engineered, not thrown together and constantly patched up. It must be acknowledged that some architectural state has always existed, but in most cases, it has existed in an unknown form or is possibly so fractured that it is incomprehensible. Through formal architectural concepts, it can now be articulated in ways previously thought impossible and lead the enterprise to prominence.

These bold new enterprises are not building some static, rigid new architecture, with a moat around the castle. Quite the opposite. They are building fluid, dynamic integrated architectures capable of evolving with the corporate strategy. A fundamental requirement of the architecture is that it must have the capability to evolve, change, and adapt. This, coupled with a renewed and frequently refreshed vision, provides keen insight into new and improved approaches. This adaptive architecture "ain't no silver bullet," but rather a "golden spike" that unites and aligns the enterprise and allows it to operate holistically and seamlessly.

The true value of the integrated architectures is not found in the architectures themselves, but in their usage throughout the enterprise. The architecture is an enabling tool whose advantage is found in how it is used, rather than the tool itself — in much the same way a carpenter uses a hammer or saw not just to nail precisely cut pieces of wood together, but to create that dream home envisioned by the owners. In a similar fashion, the business architects, strategic planners, corporate executives, and employees use these engineered architectures to create a prosperous and successful enterprise. We use the strategy, vision, initiatives, and architectures as tools to analyze current and future processes and to create and develop new capabilities, products, and services in anticipation of the marketplace, ahead of the competition, and with a passion for delighting our customers.

Few enterprises have formal and well-understood architectures, although some sort of model might exist for reference and analysis. Even in the best of models, something is missing. We get lost in the analysis and understanding of the models and get confused because things do not necessarily make sense in relation to other models. Maybe something is hidden for us to find, or worse, it is in plain sight, but we choose to ignore it. The results are a purposeless and meaningless struggle to perceive a whole from a pile of loosely associated parts. Instead, we need a purposeful and meaningful design based on a vision and developed by a committed team.

The key to making an architecture adaptive is an understanding, either through experience and know-how or through a widely accepted enterprise model. It is this design insight, experience, and know-how that we need to capture and communicate through the formal semantics and syntax of an enterprise model and make it available to the whole enterprise. Once this integrated enterprise architecture model is available, we have an opportunity for all employees to contribute ideas about new initiatives, products, and services. These benefits reap rewards not only for the enterprise, but also for the customers, stakeholders, partners, suppliers, and employees.

WHAT BENEFITS ARE DELIVERED FROM THE EBA?

Strategic Alignment

To understand the true priorities and needs of the business, you must conduct a serious strategic analysis of the enterprise. The strategy is the genesis of success. You might even consider the strategy to be the design of the corporate DNA. The data collected requires synthesis into information.

An easy way to summarize and represent the information is in a model built through some rigorous and disciplined approach. Integrated enterprise architectures illustrate the alignment of the strategy, vision, and corporate objectives with the strategic initiative road map. Finally, the strategy establishes the metrics, measures, and expectations for success from a customer-centric and stakeholder's view. You align the EBA core processes with a strategic goal and its complementary metrics and measures. When the initiatives from the strategic road map are implemented, the results must delight the customer, provide a clear competitive advantage, and improve stakeholder value.

Customer-Centric Focus

The building of the EBA from the customer-centric perspective enables the leaders to *view the enterprise holistically.* It puts the customer first and foremost, above the internal politics and functional silos. Looking at initiatives from a cost-only perspective may ignore the value to customers and cause a loss of market share. The enterprise is not about some functional organization or one of its best-selling products, but it is about its customers. Customer service and care are major differentiators in the marketplace.

Strategy to Results Connectivity

The enterprise consists of its people, processes, and technologies. Any enterprise strategic initiative must address all three and span the continuum from planning, through design, through implementation, through ongoing operations, and to ultimately predict and prove that the results achieved benefited the whole enterprise.

This evolution throughout the initiative's life cycle is purposeful, not a random occurrence or an accidental happening. The architectures and models evolve from logical to physical with an enterprise view of the imbedded base of technologies already employed. It is a matter of engineering the enterprise, not focusing on separate pieces and then force-fitting them together, but integrating and connecting all components of the value creating system by design. In addition, viewing the enterprise as an integrated group of core processes allows for decomposition and identification of the supporting and enabling component architectures.

Speed to Market

Building a new capability faster than your competitor is a desirable core competency. Thinking about a new capability earlier than the competition, envisioning the new capability, and determining how to implement it in your enterprise are also critically important. You have to achieve thought leadership along with a first-to-market presence. Understanding and knowing your corporate architectures is a key enabler for this competency.

Team Synergy

You need some common ground where leaders and employees can safely come together for enterprise visioning, critique, and analysis. You need a place where employees can freely express ideas for improvement. The architectures and models enable an exchange of different points of view with a focus on a desired result, rather than on who is doing what and how are they doing it.

It also allows for the evolution of architecture development through a growing consciousness of ideas and information exchange, rather than waiting for architectural births in a fully grown state. It enables precise communication through a graphical representation rather than a tome of difficult-to-read text. Business leaders and employees can then more easily exchange ideas and focus on initiatives that benefit the customers of the enterprise, thereby gaining a competitive advantage.

Less Rework and Waste

The EBA represents the knowledge repository of the enterprise. It illustrates what is produced, how it is produced, and who produces it. The models illustrate results and outcomes, interfaces and relationships. These items are sometimes overlooked, forgotten, or even unknown when analyzing a new initiative. With an accurate depiction of the current state, you can develop a more complete and clearly defined initiative with fewer errors of omission during the initiative's life cycle.

Continuous Improvement and Feedback

You are not done when the strategic initiative is implemented. You need a feedback loop for continuous improvement. You use the results from formal metrics and measures to make adjustments, basing actions on operational data, not opinions, guesses, or functional biases. The EBA complemented with business intelligence capabilities provides this feedback mechanism.

2

THE PROBLEM

WHAT ENTERPRISE MODELS ARE CURRENTLY AVAILABLE AND WHAT ARE THEY LIKE?

Let us say you are the brand new CEO of a midcap company. If you ask the COO, the CFO, the VP of sales, the VP of human resources, and the CIO to come to a meeting in one hour with a model of the enterprise, what do you think they will present? It is a safe bet that each would present a different model. Most assuredly, each will present accurate information and complement each discussion with a rich and descriptive dialogue. However, each will present some different view of the enterprise, just as in the famous legend of the blind men describing the elephant.[1]

If each executive were to post his respective model on the wall, it is doubtful that one model would illustrate the relationships with the other models. The executives' verbal descriptions might explain the relationships, but unless you record their conversations, most is lost after the presentation. The new CEO could *never* glean an understanding of the enterprise by simply reviewing the models on the wall and not listening to the presentations. The models are probably not consistent and not rich enough in semantics and syntax to precisely understand their meaning.

A new employee, transferring employee, or prospective employee faces this same dilemma. That is to say, a transferring employee will have to get an understanding of all the new capabilities of his new organization through a completely different model, not of the enterprise, but only of the new organization.

Some companies say they have a model or description of some aspect of their enterprise. Most likely, the model is presented at a high level and may look something like that in Figure 2.1. Some may have models with interesting and creative graphics. You might even see these in standard

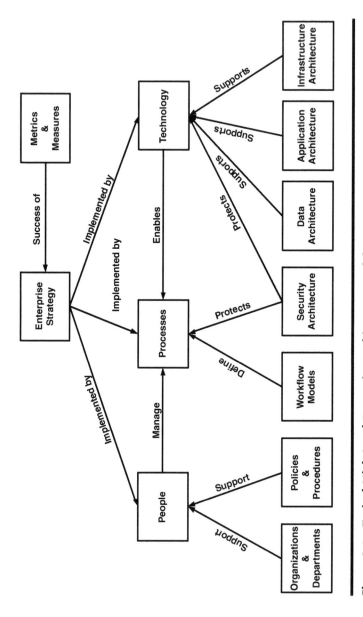

Figure 2.1 Typical High-Level Enterprise Architecture Model

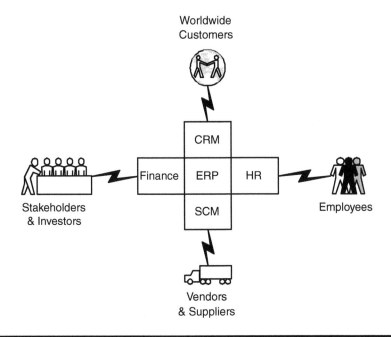

Figure 2.2   e-Business Architecture

presentations, perhaps printed on a colored poster and displayed in several offices and conference rooms.

Some information technology (IT) organizations that are exploiting Internet opportunities and looking for funding and corporate support may have developed a model similar to that in Figure 2.2. Others may have adopted something similar to the "to be" e-business application architecture described by Dr. Ravi Kalakota in *e-Business: Roadmap for Success.*[2] Here again, perhaps several excellent presentations and posters exist describing the new utopia.

Another possibility is the business function/process model described in Figure 2.3. It is defined as a set of models illustrating the functional groupings of a business. These are further subdivided into two groups: primary, which directly relate to the business of the enterprise (e.g., customer care), and supporting, which enable the primary functionality (e.g., finance). Each functional group contains several unique business processes (e.g., for finance, there are corporate accounting and asset management). This model is useful for describing the enterprise because the functions remain generally constant. The business may change its organizational structure and its processes, but the basic functions remain relatively stable. The business function/process model may very well serve other purposes, but it is most inadequate in describing the real enterprise

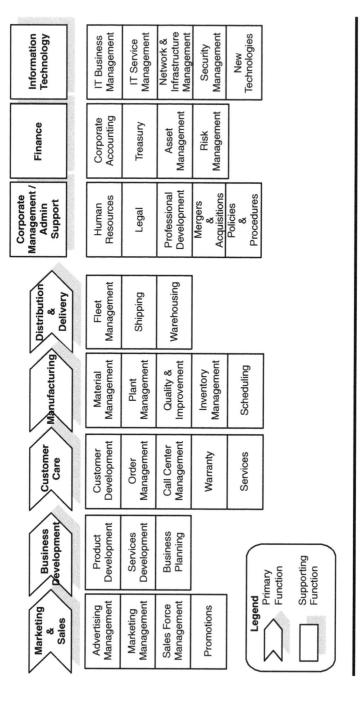

Figure 2.3   Business Function/Process Model

business architecture (EBA) and totally inadequate for integrating with the other architectures.

Now let us see what happens when we look past the aforementioned high-level models and get down to the details. A thorough review will most likely result in these findings:

- The presentation style, format, content, and descriptions vary from one organization to another.
- Very few models connect to or integrate with any other models from other organizations.
- Most are high level, abstract, and do not connect to any lower-level models.
- Most are out of date and not managed in a central repository.
- Few are actually used for any analysis of a corporate initiative.
- Few are usable in the development or maintenance of business/IT strategies and infrastructure.
- None have the same components; for example, the application architecture is missing.
- None represent the whole enterprise.
- A formal approach to modeling, building, and integrating enterprise architectures is nonexistent.

Most detailed models look like those in Figure 2.4, which present the typical characteristics of an enterprise model. The models, architectures (if any exist), and workflows are just scattered about, lacking any consistency and integration.

When it comes to undertaking a major initiative out of the corporate strategy or from a major change or opportunity in the marketplace, these models or architectures are of little or no value. Sometimes in a wild flurry of activity there is an attempt to "clean them up" and "get them updated" in a few weeks' time. This approach usually accomplishes very little.

To build any complex thing, such as a house, ship, airplane, or enterprise, you must have some sort of formal model of its structure or architecture, developed through a deliberate, disciplined engineering approach. Models and architectures are requisite for houses, ships, and airplanes, but are virtually nonexistent for business enterprises, though just as mandatory. If they do exist for an enterprise, they usually resemble the hieroglyphics typically found deep inside ancient tombs and are as indecipherable. If you do not believe this, just ask to review a model of the enterprise and see what is presented within an hour of your request. Usually it will be a marketing presentation, and once you get past the attractive high-level slides and overheads, you will find very little useful substance that can be used in research, analysis, and design. The models

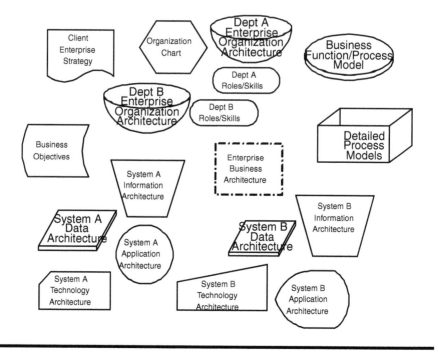

Figure 2.4   Typical Detailed Enterprise Models

and architectures that do exist are usually out of date, unreadable, not integrated, unavailable to the typical business and IT managers, and consequently are seldom used or exploited when undertaking a major new strategic initiative.

The new CEO might ask for a new enterprise model. Who will get the assignment to build the holistic enterprise model? Perhaps the CEO will turn to an outside consulting firm for model development. We do not know. What is known, however, is that to develop an acceptable enterprise model, the CEO will have to have several cross-functional teams participate in model development. To gain buy-in from the four corners of the enterprise, key participants from all functional areas, divisions, and business units will have to participate. This is a good thing. They get to participate in a highly visible project with far-reaching consequences. Participants become the voice of their functional areas or divisions. This is commendable because the CEO will get buy-in from all participants and inherent accuracy in the developed models.

To participate, each must have certain skills and attitudes. The modeling skills are teachable and learnable by almost anyone; however, the supporting rigor and discipline is another matter. For example, on one engagement during a model review session, numerous changes to a workflow were recommended. A very bright individual with excellent educational credentials but a modest amount of implementation experience was part of the team. The individual had used some modeling constructs improperly, a branch in one workflow dead-ended and another workflow did not connect properly with the enterprise business architecture. The problem needed to be corrected before proceeding any farther. It was later discovered that the consultant knew what should have been done but was only looking for a quick sign-off from the client and did not feel it was necessary to take the time to resolve the errors and shortcomings. After having the errors pointed out to him, the consultant defensively responded with, "You are just a bunch of IT guys trying to get us business guys to compile the enterprise before the requirements and analysis phase is approved and signed off!"

Although the vehemence of the retort was surprising, the observation was correct and accurate. The enterprise should and must be compiled from a requirements and analysis point of view before starting any software development, packaged software configuration, process improvement, or infrastructure expansion. Each successive life-cycle iteration should get more precise and richer in detail. What better way to reduce rework due to unclear or confusing specifications, and to ensure more of the requirements are clearly specified.

For years, the IT industry has endeavored to improve the quality of requirements and specifications. For example, we have evolved from an unstructured environment, through structured analysis and design, to object-oriented analysis and design. We have Demarco's mini-spec[3] and Jocabson et al.'s use case.[4] Each step along the way has improved our ability to determine requirements. Joint application development (JAD) sessions, conference room pilots, and the like have moved us slowly in the right direction. But what do we need and how do we build the EBA to enable the transition from strategy to results?

WHAT DO WE NEED TO MODEL THE ENTERPRISE?

Perhaps some readers are still not certain about the need for integrated architectures. After all, you probably have survived this long without them. Let us see if you have encountered this kind of situation before. It is late at night and tomorrow is your child's birthday. You open a very large box containing the child's gift and find a note in the top of the box that contains those dreaded words: "assembly required." What do you want to find next?

Many of us want a little elf to pop out and assemble it. Unfortunately, they are not packed with the gift. Instead, most of us want and need to find one of those exploded diagrams representing a three-dimensional view of all the parts fitting together along with a list of required tools. We also want some step-by-step instructions that describe how to put the

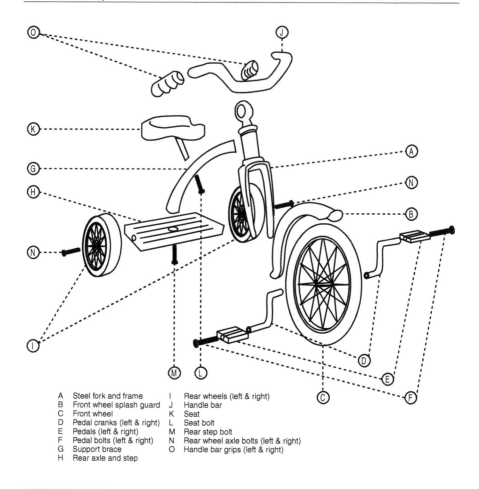

A	Steel fork and frame	I	Rear wheels (left & right)
B	Front wheel splash guard	J	Handle bar
C	Front wheel	K	Seat
D	Pedal cranks (left & right)	L	Seat bolt
E	Pedals (left & right)	M	Rear step bolt
F	Pedal bolts (left & right)	N	Rear wheel axle bolts (left & right)
G	Support brace	O	Handle bar grips (left & right)
H	Rear axle and step		

Figure 2.5   Architecture of a Gift

item together. What we need is an architecture, that three-dimensional exploded diagram, as illustrated in Figure 2.5, and its instructions to put the gift together and get it ready for your child's birthday in the morning.

As far as the need goes, the same is true for the enterprise. But in most cases, no one has documented the enterprise business architecture and packaged it neatly in a box for us to open. Therefore, we spend many needless hours trying to force-fit the enterprise together or back together after a major reorganization, merger, acquisition, or strategic planning engagement. If only we had a well-modeled EBA. In most cases comprehensive models of the enterprise just do not exist and, amazingly, are still considered unnecessary.

The next several pages will identify some typical problems and difficulties encountered during various consulting engagements. A group of the most predominant problems we found is consolidated into a concise list for analysis. For each problem, a need is identified and discussed. Seek to identify and understand the problems and needs in their totality before prematurely jumping to a solution somewhere in the middle of the analysis. The next chapter will again review the problems and needs, and then determine a solution based on a thorough understanding of all of the problems and needs.

Problem: No Formal Models of the Enterprise Exist

During typical consulting engagements, the business and IT managers are asked to provide the current models of their enterprise. Frequently, the response is, "Nothing formal is available but I can draw it on the grease board for you." If some models are available, they are usually out of date. In most cases, the architecture and workflow representations are not models at all, but simply sketches or drawings lacking any formal disciplines. These drawings merely represent the thoughts in an individual's mind and do not possess the rigor or syntax to be easily understood by others without extensive explanation.

During one engagement more than 20 IT professionals and team leaders were interviewed. Representatives from the Web teams, online teams, and batch teams presented their materials, but none presented a model using the same format as the other. There were no common schemas, constructs, or tool usage. Some depicted a piece of an architecture that somehow transitioned into a workflow, requiring multiple levels of detail to explain — sort of a multilevel "archaflow" drawing, not a real model, but just similar to a drawing of a "donkey with wings," as illustrated in Figure 2.6. A donkey with wings and a multilevel archaflow just do not exist.

A few of the presenters were unable to differentiate between architectures and workflows. There is a simple distinction provided by Ivar Jocabson et al. in *The Object Advantage*.[5] They refer to architectures as static structures, with one element linked to other elements to form, collectively, a structure. Workflows are not static, but dynamic, and a very different kind of model. Both architectures and workflows are part of the same business model, but they are different and must be integrated consistently.

How do we articulate and illustrate an enterprise model while providing a vehicle through which both dynamic and static (architectural and workflow) information is communicated?

We need a framework of models that graphically portray all major and important aspects of the enterprise.

Figure 2.6 A Donkey with Wings

We need to articulate and illustrate an enterprise model and provide a vehicle through which architectural information is communicated. In his book *Enterprise Modeling and Integration*,[6] Francois B. Vernadat defines a framework as a collection of elements put together for some purpose. It is the scope, concepts, and methods necessary for modeling enterprises. The models must have rigor and discipline surrounding their integration, relationships, and language constructs. Users of the model must have a clear understanding of the semantics and syntax of the constructs. Variation and divergence from defined standards within the framework cannot exist. Of course, it is acceptable to apply creative thinking in terms of expansion and evolution of the framework, but only through a generally accepted approval-and-release process.

Problem: An Approved Model of the Enterprise Does Not Exist

A picture is worth a thousand words. Sometimes prospective clients ask, "Why do we need a model or graphical representation of the enterprise?" Well, if you do not need one, why do so many different and varied models exist? Why do people present them as a starting point in a presentation? It seems obvious that people, in using models, are trying to communicate a lot of data and information in a short amount of time. Usually they are trying to illustrate an opportunity or maybe even a problem with a proposed solution. A model can imply a great deal of internal structure in a simple way.

Reading a text document covering the same amount of implied data will always take longer, assuming you can find the time to read it in the first place, and most likely, your interpretation will differ from those of your peers and possibly even the author. Text is also linear and not suited to reading in a nonlinear fashion. For example, do you read mystery books by starting at the last chapter?

> *We need an approved and accepted model of the enterprise, one that is holistic in nature, fully integrated, and creates unity of purpose.*

This approval, acceptance, and subsequent usage must start with the C-level executives. They must use the models consistently across and throughout the enterprise and realize that the models will require frequent updates and modifications as the enterprise evolves and matures over time. It is, however, acceptable and appropriate to make presentations of the enterprise using these models as input, but using a different format. For customer presentations, supplier meetings, or other such purposes, this is necessary. You may even want to hide some particular information to protect intellectual capital, corporate strategy, a new service offering, or a new product release. This approach provides you with some degree of flexibility while maintaining a clear link back to the base models.

Problem: An Enterprise Structure or Schema Is Undefined

Some modeling approaches represent the business using the old program flowchart notation. Others use an entity relationship diagram from a software modeling tool, or maybe an application type architecture, or maybe a network/technology type architecture. Lately, some have also used Web architectures or some variations or pieces of the application or network architectures. Some of these models are logical, but most are physical. However, none of these integrate with the EBA by design or intent.

If an EBA is modeled using the proper techniques and a modeling language that has the requisite semantics, syntax, and rigor, it is possible to directly link the business processes to the supporting and enabling IT. It is possible and preferable to integrate the IT architectures as described in *Enterprise Architecture Planning*.[7] However, most IT architectures are not even integrated internally with themselves.

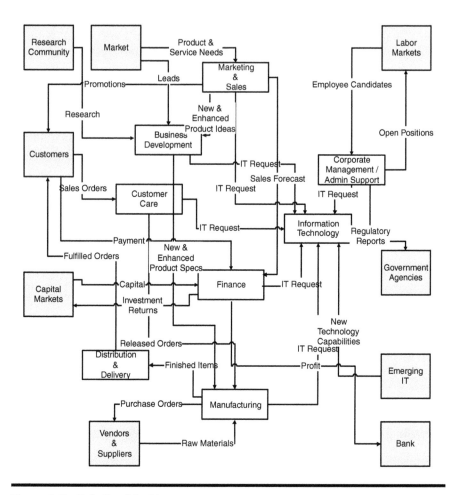

Figure 2.7   Relationship Map

We need a structure or schema to model the enterprise that allows the integration of each model with the other.

Houston, we have a problem. We do not have a generally accepted approach to building and integrating architectures and workflows. To address this problem, we need to evolve the logical models into the physical models, and then evolve them again into requirements for software creation or packaged software configuration or manual procedures. Along the way, we need the test criteria and the capability to simulate the model to verify its required expectations.

For example, consider the aforementioned business function/process model in Figure 2.3 or the relationship map in Figure 2.7. These are good models for high-level presentation purposes, being informative in nature and generally accepted. Nonetheless, neither was designed as a formal architecture with a formal link to the other enterprise architectures.

As important as the IT architectures are, these are not at the top of the hierarchy or the foundation from which evolve all other enterprise architectures. With a fully integrated set of IT architectures, you can propagate changes or enhancements from one to the other; however, you cannot adequately make the connection to the business architecture, security, or organizational architecture from a purely IT point of view.

Problem: Enterprise-wide Communications Are Ineffective

What we have here is a failure to communicate. There are numerous styles of models, some illustrating workflow and others illustrating architecture. Some even attempt to illustrate both on the same document. Each has a loosely organized set of constructs and icons with little rigor and discipline around semantics and syntax. How, then, do you communicate across the spectrums of people, processes, and technologies?

> *We need a common language, one that spans the enterprise and is comprehensible from the top to the bottom of the organization chart, that is understandable regardless of which organization, department, or division you are assigned.*

There is only one true common language: mathematics. You can reduce every enterprise down to a series of financial statements and documents found in annual reports. However, you need a sound understanding of the generally accepted accounting principles to understand and audit the numbers. Other than the annual report and a few other financial items like budgets and outlooks, the enterprise needs another better-suited language to communicate what is common between organizations, regions, divisions, business units, executives, and employees.

Problem: Understanding Enterprise Complexity

One need only consider the organizational complexity of an enterprise, with its numerous departments, hierarchies, business units, regions, divisions, and, lest we forget, all the connections to numerous external entities such as customers, suppliers, governmental regulatory agencies, and partners, to understand that an enterprise is a complex, extended, multidimensional entity.

> *We need a way to understand a complex enterprise, to break it apart for analysis and improvement and then to put it back together again, better than it was before without breaking everything else.*

Most corporate restructuring and reorganizing is conducted with a chain saw mentality. Do you remember the TV series *Home Improvement*, starring Tim Allen? He always started projects with the greatest of expectations and wound up with the most colossal failures. For a striking contrast, consider the architecture mentality and preciseness depicted in another TV series, *This Old House*, starring Norm Abram, Steve Thomas, and Tommy Silva. Using the metaphor of home-building architectures and blueprints, **this** is the concept and approach we must consider in business engineering.

Problem: Enterprise Priorities Are in Conflict

We have a riddle wrapped inside an enigma. Enterprisewide integration is very complex. Within these complex enterprises, there are conflicting priorities, objectives, and politics. Most often: "My vice-president is more powerful than your vice-president, or my department is more important than your department." We do not need the kinds of arguments that pit one department against the other. Let us save that energy and passion for dealing with the competition. Let us find a synergistic way that enables cooperation with a focus on results and outcomes, not politics and personal biases.

When asking engagement participants if the current set of priority initiatives are driven out of the business strategy, the reply usually is a cold stare or a confused "What strategy are you talking about?" Most often there is a major disconnect here. Sometimes the initiatives are based on functional priorities or organizational goals, not enterprisewide goals with supporting valid metrics and measures.

> *We need to prioritize and promptly implement those strategic initiatives that produce predictable and measurable results in the best interest of the enterprise.*

Frequently today, priorities are based on the size of the ox and the depth of the ditch it is in. Managers end work each day, bravely describing all of the fires they put out. Usually fires are destructive and costly. Management's behavior and sometimes recognition are based on containing and stopping the fire before is does too much damage. Let us try another approach. Let us prevent the fire from ever happening. Anybody can run around the enterprise with a fire extinguisher looking for a crisis to solve, but what we really want are people throughout the enterprise carrying a telescope, looking to and creating the future, a new era, anticipating and preventing problems.

Problem: A Serious Customer Focus Is Lacking

How will you grow your business, increase stakeholder value, and attract talented people? The growth of your business most likely depends on those who generate revenue for your enterprise. You may call them customers, clients, guests, patrons, or patients. For simplicity, this text will use *customer*.

> *We need a customer-centric view of the enterprise, one that puts the customer first and foremost.*

Growing your business will most likely result from the proper focus on the customer. However, after years of cost cutting through a strategic initiative called fiscal fitness, the enterprise probably has lost its customer focus, market share, and a few other things along the way. These short-term measures may turn down the heat from Wall Street, but most likely are not in the best long-term interest of the enterprise. Back-office operations are very important, but no company's dominance in its market is based on a core competency of purchasing cheap office supplies. Usually the companies that have gained a competitive advantage and dominance in their market have done so by a rigorous and purposeful focus on their customers.

When we talk about the outputs and results produced by an enterprise, we must discuss, explain, and articulate them in terms of customer value and success. Each employee must understand how his contributions to the enterprise deliver value to the customer. In some cases, these employees may serve in frontline organizations such as sales and service. In other cases, they may serve in manufacturing, procurement, or information technology. In all cases, opportunities abound for direct or indirect contributions to customer value with the proper focus.

Problem: Life Cycle/Project Phases Are Too Independent

Once an enterprise has customer focus and strategic alignment, it has a chance to track results more effectively and trace the business requirement through to the enabling technologies. Depending on which systems development methodology is used, most initiatives have a strategic phase, an analysis/design phase, a develop/implement phase, and an operational phase. Usually the corporate initiatives contain several separate, but complementary projects with overlapping phases, but in most cases the projects and phases are treated independently.

> *We need to span all life-cycle phases from strategy to results, enabling the transition from the current to the future state.*

You must progress from one project phase to another with the minimum of interpretation and translation. The days of "throwing it over the wall" are far too costly and time-consuming. Additionally, because most corporate initiatives impact a "legacy area" of the business as well as the "Web area," it makes this need even more demanding.

Considering the current state of enterprise models reviewed by the new CEO described earlier, we have just discussed what we think to be the requisite but most overlooked problems and needs to integrating enterprise architectures. These needs are by no means exclusive, and along with them should be considered leadership, commitment, and ethical professional behavior. Several excellent books address these critically important needs. One example is *The Fifth Discipline* by Peter Senge.[8] He does a superb job of integrating the five disciplines of shared vision, personal mastery, team learning, mental models, and systems thinking. Each of the five disciplines is integrated with the others, creating a whole greater than the sum of its parts. Attempting to implement or practice just one or two of the disciplines without the others is missing a tremendous opportunity.

Addressing only one or two of the needs required to build the integrated enterprise architectures exposes you to the same shortcomings as ignoring several of Senge's five disciplines. There are no quick fixes here, only the choice for a long-lasting solution. Choosing to satisfy only a few of the needs and attempting to build enterprise architectures avoiding the rest will prove futile. Eliminating a need or partially fulfilling a need may delude you into thinking that you are making some progress, but ultimately, it will prevent you from achieving the desired expectations. Ignoring two or three of the needs may also unravel the architectures and the approach. You may possibly satisfy each need differently; however, the *fulfillment of the need is a requirement*. If you are going to build a useful and robust enterprise business architecture, then build it by applying the right approach in its entirety.

REFERENCES

1. Karen Backstein, *The Blind Men and the Elephant* (New York: Scholastic, 1992).
2. Dr. Ravi Kalakota and Marcia Robinson, *e-Business: Roadmap for Success* (Reading, MA: Addison-Wesley Longman, 1999), 103.
3. Tom Demarco, *Structured Analysis and System Specification* (New York: Prentice Hall, 1979), 343 (foreword by P.J. Plauger).
4. Ivar Jocabson, Maria Ericsson, and Agneta Jacobson, *The Object Advantage: Business Process Reengineering with Object Technology* (Reading, MA: Addison-Wesley, 1995), 343.
5. Ibid., 31–33.
6. Francois B. Vernadat, *Enterprise Modeling and Integration: Principles and Applications* (New York: Chapman & Hall 1996), 32.
7. Steven H. Spewak and Steven C. Hill, *Enterprise Architecture Planning: Developing a Blueprint for Data, Applications and Technology* (Wellesley, MA: QED Publishing Group, 1993), 224 (foreword by John A. Zachman).
8. Peter M. Senge, *The Fifth Discipline: The Art & Practice of the Learning Organization* (New York: Doubleday, 1990), 6–10.

3

THE SOLUTION

WHAT IS AN INTEGRATED ENTERPRISE ARCHITECTURE?

Before discussing in detail the analysis of the needs, we need to clarify a few terms and definitions. We also need to provide a little insight into the solution, or at least a peek at the answer. Let us first define and agree on the general definition for an integrated enterprise architecture. The following definitions should be taken under advisement:

- An architecture is defined as the structure of components, their relationships, and the principles and guidelines governing their design and evolution over time.[1]
- Enterprise architectures are like blueprints, drawings, or models.[2]
- Enterprise architectures refer to an organized set of elements with clear relationships to one another, which together form a whole defined by its finality.[3]

Each provides a good definition of architecture and is reasonably understood by both business and information technology (IT) professionals. If applied properly, each unifies the enterprise by bringing all parts together to create a whole. These definitions also imply precise alignment and connectivity, through a systematic approach, rather than a seat-of-the-pants approach. For this text we have developed the following definition:

Integrated enterprise architectures define the style and method of design and construction that comprise the elements of a system and define the purposes and interrelationships of those elements.

In all cases, the following is a fundamental precept:

Architectures illustrate the relationships between parts that create a whole; however, they do not illustrate flow, sequence, or timing of events.

IT architectures may reference a business architecture, but should seldom define one. Although there are many definitions in the industry for each of the enterprise IT architectures, a generally accepted, standard definition, understanding, or description of an enterprise business architecture (EBA) does not exist. Just ask three or four fellow employees to define an EBA and see how much variety you get in their descriptions.

Many attempts have been made to derive a business architecture out of the IT architectures. For those who believe that technology drives business, this is typical behavior. In reality, business should drive the use of technology and technology should focus on enabling the business. How could you ever build that dream home by starting with the electrical and plumbing architectures and let them define the outcome? How could you ever build an airplane by starting with the flight control system without first determining if the requirement is for a commercial airliner or a military fighter?

Technology in and of itself will not save us, nor will that next "hot" Web project. Historically, the technology-alone view has disappointed us many times before. For example, remember the hyped-up expectations of structured analysis methodologies, client/server technologies, object-oriented methodologies, and the Internet? A similar situation was described in the July 1, 2003, issue of *CIO* magazine.[4] The article states, "IT has not delivered on its promises to the enterprise." Ultimately, the business was disappointed with the technology-alone expectations and IT's return on investment — so much so that when the next round of technology "greatness" came along, we had to oversell its expectations to overcome the previous disappointments. If anything will save us, it is the business strategy integrated with the business and technology initiatives, implemented within an adaptive architecture.

Sometimes the business architecture is defined or described by a business function/process model, which is functionally centric. Refer to Figure 2.3. Some consultants start with a business function/process model and then try to draw connecting lines between the vertical functions to various processes to describe a core cross-functional process within the business architecture. Using the business function/process model in this manner will eventually cause you to lose track of the purpose and value of each function/process.[5] When asking fellow IT associates and business people "What is a business architecture?" the usual replies are vague and contain very broad descriptions, and no two people have ever drawn or sketched out a similar graphical representation. Some even start out with a corporate organization chart and make a futile attempt to use it to describe their interpretation of a business architecture.

So let us define an enterprise business architecture and its major components:

> An **enterprise business architecture** defines the enterprise value streams and their relationships to all external entities and other enterprise value streams and the events that trigger instantiation. It is a definition of what the enterprise must produce to satisfy its customers, compete in a market, deal with its suppliers, sustain operations, and care for its employees. It is composed of models of architectures, workflows, and events.

> A **value stream** is an end-to-end collection of activities that creates a result for a customer, who may be the ultimate customer or an internal end user of the value stream. The value stream has a clear goal: to satisfy or to delight the customer.[6]

Having just defined integrated enterprise architectures and the enterprise business architecture, we need to look closer at the EBA to gain a cursory understanding of its basic conceptual structure.

First of all, you may want to know where the EBA fits in the overall view of the corporate value system. Refer to Figure 1.1. The EBA is a foundational architecture that links up to the corporate strategy and business environment and down to the other enterprise architectures, process initiatives, software development domains, and package configuration domains. If you have attempted to integrate architecture and software/package development back to the strategy to set the priority of corporate initiatives and to prove the value of IT, you realize how difficult this is and how loose and imprecise the connections are.

Herein lies the basic purpose and value of the well-defined EBA. You can "hard wire" all of the connections, integration, and touchpoints by applying the concepts of an EBA to your enterprise. Just think, no more loose connections, but a direct connection between a corporate strategic initiative, a value stream in the EBA, and the supporting effort to implement a predicable performance improvement. No other architecture, model, diagram, drawing, or hieroglyphic will make all the connections. You cannot do this with the application architecture, the business function/process model, or the organization chart. Many presentations allude to the integration and connectivity back to the corporate strategy, but that is usually as far as it goes: an allusion. There is nothing of substance available

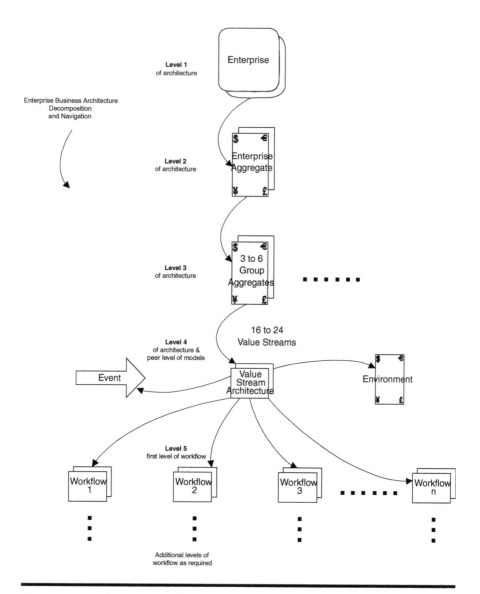

Figure 3.1 Basic Conceptual Structure of the EBA

to support the colorful slides in the presentation. What we need is an integrating architecture between the corporate strategy and the other architectures and initiatives.

Inside of the enterprise business architecture box, as previously indicated in Figure 1.1, you must find a true representation of the business that will allow you to integrate and hard wire the corporate linkages as illustrated in Figure 3.1.

The high-level depiction of the basic EBA structure (Figure 3.1) provides a conceptual overview of the major components and the integration schema. With the balanced and leveled inputs and outputs produced by the various processes, you can integrate and develop the EBA — its *architectures, workflows,* and *events.* This basic structure illustrates how all of the models fit together to form a harmonious whole for the enterprise. This approach also allows us to focus on specific models for analysis while understanding their relationships to the rest of the enterprise.

For example, your team may decide to focus on one specific strategic objective. All strategic objectives are linked to the enterprise value streams with supporting metrics and measures. You then begin to analyze how the value streams impact your particular objective and what improvements are necessary to realize the strategic expectations. The results of your analysis may require process improvement, infrastructure expansion, or software development in one or more of the value streams. The enhancements are modeled in the appropriate workflows, and this information becomes input to the strategic initiative and its project plan. Depending on the nature and scope of the plan, you may have any combination of project tasks associated with process improvement, infrastructure expansion, or software development. Each task is driven from a single source of knowledge, the enhanced workflows in the EBA. You determine the requirements for each project task from the EBA, thereby hard wiring the integration from strategy to results. We will demonstrate the particulars of how this comes about later.

If you want to see a more detailed example of the EBA, refer to Figure 6.1. This is a classroom workshop example of a real EBA. It illustrates all types of models and their connectivity and integration with one another. For presentation purposes, the *Order-to-Cash* value stream is presented in the middle of the example, showing its aggregation up to the *enterprise entity* (a representation of the entire business enterprise) and its decomposition down to the first level of workflows. The upcoming chapters will build up to this example.

As for the other architectures, *technology, security,* and *organization,* their integration and derivation are also enabled with the same balanced and leveled inputs and outputs, initially identified and defined in the EBA. It should be noted that the EBA inputs and outputs, which are common to all architectures, provide the business-driven touchpoints and links to all other architectures. Thus, it is critical to know and understand the inputs and outputs of all processes and activities to solidify the integration. Of course, other rationalized and synthesized information as well as approaches and disciplines are required to complete the integration with the other architectures.

As necessary and important as the inputs and outputs are, you also must have some sort of foundation to support the classification and organization of the activities. Some consultants use business functions, and others use the core processes of some specific interest; however, both of these choices provide only a fragmented view of the enterprise. For the EBA, the *value streams* are the organizing and unifying principle in the foundation. We classify and organize individual models in the EBA principally based on their value stream assignment. They give you a complete and holistic view of the enterprise with a focus on the end result or outcome.

As you can deduce, we have massive amounts of information about the enterprise captured in the EBA and we need to communicate it across the four corners of the enterprise. We need to make it available to executives for high-level planning, to midlevel managers for operational control, and to individual teams for execution. Accepting the points stated above, how, then, do you communicate this extensive amount of information to the enterprise? There are not enough PowerPoint presentations, models, diagrams, drawings, or wall posters available or coherent enough in the typical enterprise to achieve this communications imperative.

To begin an effective communication process, all models in the EBA must use a standard notation or *common modeling language*, not a potpourri of different models and miscellaneous constructs. Other architectures may have different methodologies, modeling languages, and constructs, but within each architecture, you must have consistency and discipline. To derive one architecture domain and integrate it with another, you must have shared relationships. We use the balanced and leveled inputs and outputs defined in the EBA as the vinculum between the numerous and various cross-functional processes.

There must also be a consistent way of collecting and organizing information. Through the method of *decomposition*, we can classify all of the tasks, activities, functions, and processes into value streams. We can then aggregate or classify the value streams based on the nature of our enterprise. Through this classification process, we create a hierarchy. We determine the hierarchy based on the unique characteristics of our enterprise, but there are some generally accepted levels that we use for consideration and analysis. The multiple levels of the hierarchy are similar to a bill of materials used in manufacturing a product. The enterprise's equivalent bill of materials or bill of processes essentially translates into a classification of the enterprise's components, and hence the development of a component architecture or service-oriented architecture.

We obviously need to evolve our enterprise rather than let it mutate uncontrollably. We control evolution and build-out of the enterprise with the *enterprise strategy*, which is essentially the corporate DNA. For strategic planning purposes, we need rigorously developed enterprise architecture models for analysis and future design. The strategists need these models to reach consensus on the selection of new initiatives or the termination of ineffective ones. The EBA, both the current state and future state, provides the holistic view of the enterprise for this analysis, rather than perpetuating arguments on "which blind man's view of the elephant" is more critical to the success of the enterprise.

Throughout the EBA, the numerous inputs and outputs are mapped illustrating their sources and destinations to other external entities as well. We must focus on getting goods and services to our customers and therefore primarily viewing the enterprise from the *customer's perspective*. The customer and other external entities, such as our stakeholders, partners, and suppliers, are critical to developing a comprehensive EBA that we will use to improve the performance of the enterprise. The completion of a strategic initiative must deliver the expected improvements and ultimately make our customers happier and more satisfied.

Once we have used the EBA to develop some strategic initiatives, we need to implement them efficiently. We usually employ cross-functional teams in the initiative. We also need a life-cycle methodology to direct the implementation of the initiative. Throughout the life cycle, from *strategy to results,* we need to transition from one project phase to the next with a minimum of confusion. The EBA build-out and its integration with the other architectures ensure that all affected people, processes, and technologies are accounted for and evolve in accordance with expectations, from the current state to the future state.

It must be emphasized that the EBA is an engineering type diagram, not a sketch or drawing. As its development matures, it gets richer in detail, more accurate, and becomes a better reflection of the operational enterprise. In addition, it has a customer focus, based on a holistic view of the enterprise. You can evolve and derive other architectures from the EBA base, improve the critical performance measures, and transition to the first iteration of Unified Modeling Language (UML)/Rational Unified Process (RUP) development or initial packaged software configuration. It is not a throwaway model, but an evolving model, hardwired to the corporate strategy and vision. Its basic purpose is to unify the enterprise, improve its effectiveness and efficiency, and eventually produce the value-creating system as defined in the corporate strategy.

As you will see in the remaining chapters, the EBA structure (see Figure 3.1) will slowly come into focus. It will evolve out of the analysis of corporate needs and a desire to seek out a true solution to the typical enterprise problems. Some readers will prefer to "just get to the answer." However, we have found that it is better to share some thoughts and ideas with an audience, rather than just throw out an answer or proposal. For those who prefer to forgo the analysis chapter, we suggest that you

Table 3.1 Enterprise Modeling Needs

What do we need?	*How do we satisfy the need?*
A framework of models that graphically portray all major and important aspects of the enterprise.	The framework of models consists of *architectures, workflows, and events,* integrated with one another using an engineering type discipline.
An approved and accepted model of the enterprise, one that is holistic in nature, fully integrated, and creates unity of purpose.	There are *four basic or foundational logical architectures* from which all other physical architectures are evolved or are a subset.
A structure or schema to model the enterprise that allows the integration of each model with the other.	The organizing principle for integration is an enterprise business architecture hierarchy based on *value streams.*
A common language, one that spans the enterprise and is comprehensible from the top to the bottom of the organization chart, that is understandable regardless of which organization, department, or division you are assigned.	The communications medium for creating a shared understanding between people, processes, and technologies requires a *common modeling language* rich in constructs that can describe the enterprise's framework of models in precise and clear terms.
To understand a complex enterprise, to break it apart for analysis and improvement, and then put it back together again, better than it was before and without breaking everything else.	To analyze complex enterprises, apply the *basic principles of decomposition* around both processes and data.
To prioritize and promptly implement those strategic initiatives that produce predictable and measurable results in the best interest of the enterprise.	An *enterprise strategy* with its strategic initiative road map provides insight and direction based on the return on investment.
A customer-centric view of the enterprise, one that puts the customer first and foremost.	The enterprise must first measure its success from *the customer's point of view.*
To span all life-cycle phases from planning through operations, enabling the transition from the current to the future state.	Any enterprise initiative must consider the iterative nature of business cycles, integrating people, processes, and technologies from *strategy to results.*

skip to the next chapter to see how we put it all together and later develop a case study.

HOW DO YOU SATISFY THE NEEDS REQUIRED FOR BUILDING THE ARCHITECTURES AND MODELS?

The following section will describe in greater detail how each need is fulfilled for building and modeling an enterprise business architecture. As each need is analyzed, you may notice a reference to another need. This illustrates the linkage and connectivity, or nexus, with other components in the approach. The reader may have to reread or review this section to understand the interdependencies of the EBA approach. With all of the interrelationships, there is no real sequential order to fulfilling the needs, and we have numbered them only for presentation purposes.

Once you understand some of the basic definitions and precepts, you will find that other components of the approach build, complement, and expand one upon another. You will also find references to needs that are not yet described. A little patience is required not only to fully grasp the concept but also to understand the consequences of the ways the needs are satisfied. This approach is not linear or sequential, but cyclic in nature, with no real beginning or end. To coin an old quality phrase, this is not an arrival at a destination, but the beginning of a journey.

TABLE OF NEEDS

The needs that must be met and fulfilled for building and modeling an enterprise business architecture are summarized in Table 3.1. The ensuing discussion in the following sections will provide additional explanations and descriptions as to the choice made to satisfy the need.

A FRAMEWORK OF MODELS

Table 3.2   Need: A Framework of Models

What do we need?	How do we satisfy the need?
A framework of models that graphically portray all major and important aspects of the enterprise.	The framework of models consists of *architectures, workflows, and events,* integrated with one another using an engineering type discipline.

Terms and Definitions

A **framework** refers to a collection of elements put together for some purpose.[7] The EBA framework requires models of architectures, workflows, and events all integrated one with another.

Building integrated architectures requires a very formal framework. The framework and approach are simple in nature but require a rigorous discipline in adherence to structure and execution of approach. The rigor and discipline enable you to expand your thinking in a controlled manner and to view the enterprise holistically with a customer-centric view.

The EBA framework includes three elemental types of enterprise models:

- *Architectures* — Graphically portray the style and method of design and construction that comprise the elements of an enterprise and define the purpose and interrelationships of those elements. *Architectures are static models that show relationships between workflows and do not illustrate flows or sequences.*
- *Workflows* — Graphically portray how inputs are transformed to outputs for the enterprise. Workflows illustrate the flow of control, delays, sequencing, and which entity performs the activity. *Workflows are dynamic models that require activation by an event.*
- *Events* — Graphically portray when the enterprise must react in a preplanned way. Events initiate workflows in the architecture. *Events trigger actions or processes in the enterprise.*

With these somewhat different elements (static models, dynamic models, and triggers), you have to find a way to integrate and connect them both internally and externally. This linkage is established through the strict discipline of defining all external inputs and outputs for all modeled activities and processes. *These inputs and outputs are the unifying bond between the processes* in very much the same way that bolts, cables, ports, and fitted connectors enable the assembly of a PC. The architecture, workflow, and event models are all required, with balanced and leveled external inputs and outputs.

In *Enterprise Modeling with UML*, Chris Marshall[8] describes the convergence of business, information, and natural systems thinking into the new discipline of **business engineering**. This convergence of architectures is enabled with balanced and leveled external inputs and outputs. We need to develop and evolve the business, its enabling software, and its supporting organizational roles into a single integrated system.

Observations and Findings

Most typical business modeling approaches create only workflows. Usually the workflows start at a functional level, although some start at the very bottom of a business process, and a few even include the event models. In most cases the workflows are not balanced and leveled with the external inputs and outputs, and in almost all cases, the architecture models (the static models that show relationships between workflows) are missing.

However, to view the enterprise holistically, you must have all three types of models: architectures, workflows, and event models. The architectures must clearly define the relationships between all components of the enterprise through the external inputs and outputs. The architectures, workflows, and business events are all required to bring the models to closure and some reasonable state of finality.

In one presentation given as part of an in-house reengineering effort, the classroom was awash with models of all sorts. A small book of documentation was also located on each table. Many participants arrived early and began to review the walls and documentation. Within five minutes, most were totally lost in the maze of models. As they sought understanding from the models on the walls, some began to feel that they were looking at an airplane crash site. Perhaps all the parts were there, but where was the airplane?

The subsequent presentation was not much better; however, it did improve the understanding of the models with handholding from the various presenters. Far too much time was spent explaining what the models were trying to communicate, and too little time analyzing the models' performance expectations. At one point in the presentation, someone asked if the model on the overhead was an architecture or a workflow. The presenter stumbled, flip-flopped the response, and finally answered that it was really both (another donkey with wings archaflow). The presenter was confused as well.

Most of the confusion that arises in model types occurs between architectures and workflows. Basically, **architectures** are static models representing relationships. **Workflows** are dynamic models representing transformations of inputs to outputs or changes of state. *A relationship between two workflows is expressed in an architecture.*

For example, in the Order-to-Cash value stream, you have some workflows (or business use cases), one called "fulfill order" and another called "change order." Each is different in its workflow, has a different purpose, and is initiated by a different event. One illustration of a relationship between the two is the order in the order repository. You must have placed the order in the first event before you can change it in a second event. The order information is common between the two work-flows and the "change order" is dependent on the "fulfill order." This relationship is illustrated in the value stream architecture. To describe all of the tasks and activities in "fulfill order" without understanding all of the tasks and activities in "change order" and other workflows in the value stream architecture, one risks developing incomplete or incorrect business requirements. For example, you cannot change a previously completed order.

The workflow illustrates what is and is not allowed per the business rules. The validation of any business rule is illustrated by an output or even possibly an input. For example, you may validate a customer bill with the original order, the order confirmation, or the order receipt, which are outputs and inputs. You may also validate an order rejection due to, say, "credit limit exceeded" or some other specified rejection business rule.

Rationale and Justification

As the architectures are decomposed, each is balanced and leveled with the higher-level models. Then as one starts to derive and develop another architecture, the consistency and integration are maintained between architectures via the inputs and outputs. These balanced and leveled inputs and outputs are critical between architectures. Without them, your con-necting links are broken and your integration severely compromised. This keeps all architectures hardwired together, as illustrated in Figure 3.2. The architectures integrate the workflows initiated by the external business events. For example, can you walk from one room in your home to another? Only if the architect designed and built a door. The same concept is true for an enterprise.

The lowest-level business architectural component represents the tran-sition point to the first level of workflow. This first-level workflow is a business use case as described in *The Rational Unified Process* by Philippe Kruchten.[9] The business use case model describes high-level business processes and provides the context and source of information for express-ing the system's use cases. In business modeling, we use the same concept of use case (as defined in UML) but at the level of the whole business rather than only the system under consideration.

Architecture decomposition eventually transitions to workflows or busi-ness use cases. Continue to decompose the enterprise, its value streams, and its architectural models until each of its components or business use cases achieves some relative independence from the other business use cases. Then cross-check the independent business use cases to see if each is directly associated with an event external to the enterprise or value stream. You are now ready for workflow development, analysis, and decomposition.

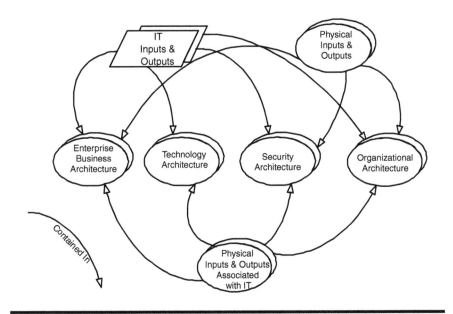

Figure 3.2 Shared Input and Output Relationships

Events represent any solicited or unsolicited happenings of the enterprise requiring some processing.[10] Events are external, internal, synchronized, and temporal. Events initiate business use cases (or workflows) defined in the architecture. The same rules of decomposition and aggregation apply here as well. For example, the event "customer places order" is an aggregate of the lower-level events called "customer places order with credit card" and "customer places order with cash." And by the way, if you have a defined event, you must have a business use case within the value stream architecture. A workflow without an event may represent an event omission or an unnecessary workflow.

You can classify all of the needed models into one of three categories: **architectures**, **workflows**, and **events**. Of course, you may supplement these models with other diagrams or drawings, but basically the information must be represented by one of the three types. You may even choose to reformat some of the models for presentation purposes, but they should always have a basis in the actual models.

Considerations and Recommendations

The value stream and logical software component matrix is very useful in presentations about the application architecture; refer to Figure 3.3 as an illustration. Some might call this a variation of the application architecture. This matrix is a static model, illustrating relationships between

Value Streams and Logical Software Components Matrix

Value Streams:
1. Prospect to Customer
2. Order to Cash
3. Manufacturing to Distribution
4. Request to Service
5. Insight to Strategy
6. Vision to eBusiness Enterprise
7. Concept to Development
8. Initiative to Results
9. Relationship to Partnership
10. Forecast to Plan
11. Requisition to Payables
12. Resource Availability to Consumption
13. Acquisition to Obsolescence
14. Financial Close to Reporting
15. Recruitment to Retirement
16. Awareness to Prevention

Group	Logical Software Component	1. Prospect to Customer
Distribution & Delivery	Supply Schedule Mgmt	
	Supply Chain Mgmt	
	Logistics	✕
	Shipping	
Operations	Manufacturing	✕
	Engineering	
	Quality Management	
	Inventory	
	Capacity Management	
	Product Configuration	✕
	Work Flow Mgmt	
	Work In Progress	
	Bill of Materials	
	Scheduling	✕
Customer Care	Cust Relationship Mgmt	
	Complaint Management	
	Service Management	✕
	Call Management	✕
Sales	Enterprise Cust Mgmt	✕
	Broker Commission	
	Sales Commission	
	Order Entry	✕
Marketing	Advertising	
	Sales & Marketing	
Information Technology	Systems Management	
	Mail/GroupWare Mgmt	
	FAX Mgmt	✕
	Web Mgmt	✕
Financial	Cost Management	
	Budgeting/Outlooks	
	Cash Management	
	General Ledger	
	Fixed Asset Mgmt	
	Accounts Payable	
	Purchasing	
	Accounts Receivable	✕
Corporate Mgmt / Administrative Support	Training	
	Time Mgmt	
	Payroll	
	Human Resources	

Figure 3.3 Value Stream and Logical Software Component Matrix Example

value streams and logical software components, summarized (or aggregated) for presentation purposes. This matrix is also useful in determining what software components might be impacted with a change to a particular value stream or other related value streams.

You may take one of the logical software components, "accounts receivable" under the financial aggregation, for example, and decompose it farther down into subfunctions such as credit checking, billing, dunning, and collections. This logical software component may represent a functional component with subcomponents or an object-oriented component with methods. However, the matrix does not, nor is it intended to, contain the numerous inputs and outputs of the components that are contained in the business architecture and logical application architecture models. Nonetheless, this matrix is an architecture type, with less detailed information, but still appropriate. With the necessary rigor and discipline, you can easily keep it hardwired to the other more detailed models.

The same holds true for a CRUD (create, retrieve, update, delete) matrix. This type of matrix illustrates the relationships between business functions and data entities. Here again, you may choose to decompose or aggregate either functions or data for your particular purpose, all the while keeping the matrix hardwired to the business architecture, logical data/information architecture, and logical application architecture.

For presentation purposes, you may take a business use case model and eliminate some of the inputs and outputs. This is particularly effective if discussing an important or critical aspect of the workflow with a peer team modeling another workflow. Using this type of model for presentation purposes speeds up communications. After making your point, encourage the peer team to refer back to the "real" model and eventually discard the presentation model.

Using the real model as input to a presentation is highly recommended. However, people sometimes do not understand the need for the two types of models. Some think that you are strictly prohibited from using anything other than the real models. This is simply not true. You need to do what makes sense for getting your point across. Just ensure that the presentation uses the real model as its foundation. It is perfectly OK to hide or eliminate detail for your presentation. You may also use different shapes and colors, or make other similar changes. Sometimes confidentiality and protection of intellectual property are necessary as well. Just do not expect your presentation model to substitute for a real model because you had a well-received presentation.

Enterprise use case models must illustrate who, what, where, how, and when. Although these models represent the possible workflow variations, they are not intended to represent the execution of every unique workflow instantiation or occurrence within the business architecture. You will not find in each value stream a unique use case model for all the possibilities that might occur in the business world. For example, you will find a workflow model containing a branch describing two possible outcomes, but you will not find two separate, unique use cases in the EBA. However, you will find these use cases in the UML software development domain.

For validation purposes, you can build real-life scenarios of possibilities using the business architecture as input and using the events as the major building blocks of assembly. Some people call these scenarios, system test cases, or user acceptance test cases. These are sometime used in joint application development (JAD) sessions or conference room pilots. You may also use an extensive set of these scenarios to "compile the enterprise" in hopes of identifying any omitted or confusing requirements.

You may even set up performance criteria for the management of these scenarios, even linking the metrics and measures back to the corporate strategy. This improves the ability of managers to meet and exceed their performance expectations defined in the objectives of the corporate strategy. These real-life test case scenarios are critically important, but are not found as workflow models in the business architecture. Additionally, you will not find a management model of a workflow in the business architectures. Management of a workflow is appropriately tracked with a schedule. Here again, both the creation of real-life scenarios and the management of a workflow are outside the domain of the business architecture.

When developing test cases, use the events as the starting point. For example, initiate a "fulfill order" workflow, change the item quantity before the order is scheduled in the "change order" workflow, and then verify the change in "review order." You will use the events to invoke a series of workflows in the architecture. The successful completion of the scenario depends on the defined set of circumstances established to test the business requirements, not unlike what happens in the business world during daily operations. As you can see, you can develop thousands of possibilities and thousands of test cases in a short amount of time.

By encapsulating the workflows in self-contained units of work or components, and integrating them through the architecture, you can support an almost infinite number of real-world scenarios or possibilities as per the business requirements. These self-contained units of work contain all of the people, process, and technology elements necessary for integration. In addition, this component approach to architecture allows you to integrate and develop capabilities from a holistic point of view rather than cobbling together several incompatible workflows in an on-the-fly fashion. You might even call this business engineering. You may have noticed the similarity between self-contained workflows and objected-oriented concepts. This is not by accident, but rather by design. This provides the integrating and linking capability to UML.

As previously stated, most enterprises do have numerous workflow models, some extending for pages in either a vertical or horizontal "swim lane" format. However, most enterprises do not have a business architecture that integrates and connects all of the workflows. Sometimes there are references to the triggering events, but not in all models. In reality, the business architecture is seldom modeled, but only implied in the IT architectures. Without the models, you just have to accept the integration on faith, or your intuitive understanding is only confirmed through presentations and discussions.

In many cases we have IT experts with a detailed and thorough understanding of an enterprise or vertical industry who are able to develop and build the IT architectures based on their years of experience and industry insight. Some of these IT experts will present a high-level view of some part of the business architecture to provide validation for a particular initiative and perhaps show where the IT architecture fits within the enterprise. Unfortunately, this information is locked in the minds of these experts and is not modeled in an appropriate or disciplined fashion that can be used by lesser-skilled technicians or even business personnel.

If you do not have a formal, holistic business architecture that is fully integrated with the workflows and events, what do you have? Where do the models reside and how are they maintained? We have to ask, Where will we maintain the knowledge repository of the enterprise? Will we maintain it in the minds of the employees with all of its variations, or will we formally model it for analysis and examination? It is a tough decision. We have to decide to stay put or to move ahead.

Do you have numerous workflow models? Are they connected through an architecture model? Do you capture the events?

AN ACCEPTED ENTERPRISE MODEL

Table 3.3   Need: An Accepted Enterprise Model

What do we need?	How do we satisfy the need?
An approved and accepted model of the enterprise, one that is holistic in nature, fully integrated, and creates unity of purpose.	There are *four basic or foundational logical architectures* from which all other physical architectures are evolved or are a subset.

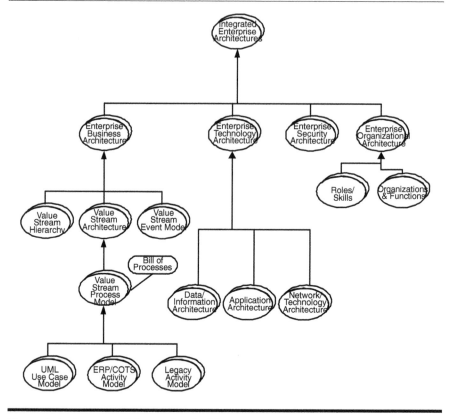

Figure 3.4   Integrated Enterprise Architectures

Terms and Definitions

There are four basic logical architectures that comprise the enterprise architecture, each tightly integrated to make the whole. These architectures are the enterprise business architecture, the enterprise technology architecture, the enterprise security architecture, and the enterprise organizational architecture. Usually the data/information, application, and network/technology (infrastructure) architectures are collectively referred to as the technology architecture. Each of the enterprise architectures is addressed individually for discussion purposes. There certainly may be other models and architectures, but these represent the foundation from which to evolve, build, and integrate all others. Refer to Figure 3.4. Definitions are provided for each.

Enterprise Business Architecture

The EBA defines the enterprise value streams and their relationships to all external entities and other enterprise value streams and the events that trigger instantiation. The EBA serves as the central plexus of the enterprise.

It is a definition of what the enterprise must produce to satisfy its customers, compete in a market, deal with its suppliers, sustain operations, and care for its employees. It is comprised of architectures, workflows, and events.

A business architecture also reflects an enterprise view of what the business must do today as well as in the future to accomplish particular business requirements. This view is based on the business context and the guidance provided by strategic business plans. The EBA additionally characterizes the business organization structure and the enterprise operating environment within which all integrated enterprise architectures exist. It is the business context and business architecture that will provide the rationale for the future enterprise IT, security, and organization architectures' baseline and development.

The EBA will be used for understanding and assessing the business processes (value streams), identifying opportunities, indicating the required construction of supporting physical architectures to achieve desired business goals, and effectively identifying how information technology can enable an enterprise to meet its business objectives.

The enterprise business operating environment provides a high-level overview of the environment for identifying and designing the IT architectures. This characterization allows for:

- Developing a business and information technology alignment perspective
- Identifying and designing the logically integrated enterprise business and IT architectures, and understanding the enterprise information and systems environment requirements to include system continuity, and physical and data security requirements
- Defining the logical and geographical requirements for the data/information, application, network/technology infrastructure, security, and organization architectures

Data/Information Architecture

This architecture identifies and defines the major kinds of data that support the business functions defined in the business model. The definitions become the standards to be subsequently used for logical database design, physical database design, and database creation.[11] The information architecture requires that the enterprise stop developing isolated or independent databases and start designing common, up-to-date, shared, distributed, and consistent data repositories.

A data architecture defines the data, at an element level, its associated relationships, in what processes they are used and in what form, and how they flow between processes. An information architecture, on the other hand, is abstracted at a level higher and identifies the informational needs of the enterprise in the context of core business processes and strategic goals of the enterprise. In other words, an information architecture represents what information must be delivered to individuals across the enterprise to help them effectively execute business processes and make informed decisions.

The information architecture does not identify data elements or detailed processes, but rather identifies what operational and decision support systems are needed to support the core processes and strategic goals, where the information for those systems is located, and how this information will be managed. It also contains the information and data management framework and precepts; the models for the integrated information, application, and technology architectures; and the information-applications software portfolio that addresses business intelligence scenarios.

A major purpose of the information architecture is to provide the business intelligence structure, or feedback loop, to give employees the ability to analyze the performance of a business and its capability to achieve the business goals, objectives, critical success factors, and performance metrics outlined in the enterprise strategic business plan.

The information architecture is the cornerstone of an organization's ability to effectively manage information. This capability is critical to the discovery and exploration of information related to the crucial factors and trends of a business and its industry.

Application Architecture

The application architecture is a catalog of applications along with the functions that they deliver and interfaces between applications. The application architecture is also mapped against the data architecture. The application is cross-referenced with one or more data items that it creates, retrieves, updates, or deletes.[12]

An application architecture serves to support business process execution and brings information and data to the process. The application architecture defines the application software portfolio and integration relationships. Technically, it defines interface specifications, tools, utilities, and, in some cases, approved products for applications. It also provides a common environment in which applications can operate, thus providing selection criteria, improving interoperability, and reducing application maintenance complexity. Application inputs and outputs are identified, as well as the application geographical deployment requirements. Guiding principles, standards, and design characteristics support the acquisition as well as development of applications.

Its purpose is to provide a logical portfolio of applications for supporting the various business processes of an enterprise. The application portfolio is designed to illustrate the optimum distribution of applications and components across multiple business functions, processes, sites, and platforms for enabling business workflow scenarios that will ensure efficient and effective business operations.

Network/Technology Architecture

This architecture defines the major kinds of technologies needed to provide an environment for the applications that are managing data. It defines the kinds of technologies referred to as platforms, or infrastructure, that will support the business with a shared data environment. Technology platforms are the pipeline and physical facilities of a data utility.[13]

A network/technology architecture enables access to information and provides support for the execution of activities. This framework contains the standards and policies or "building codes" for infrastructure construction. This framework also contains the logical location software deployment schemas as well as a characterization of the infrastructure environment to provide the baseline for the target environment. It also provides identification and views of the future geographical layouts with IT platform operating requirements and characteristics that will provide the basis for engineering blueprints and deployment.

The enterprise network/technology architecture provides the technology structure to support the information, application architectures, and systems management practices. The network/technology architecture describes the underlying systems and associated platforms to integrate the business intelligence and business application portfolios into an enterprise information system.

As part of the infrastructure, enterprise IT management provides for the exchange of IT systems management information with information technology systems and services within a corporation's enterprise. Additionally, it provides the structure to define optimum value to the client by defining demand, products and services, fulfillment of demand, and the planning and managing of all aspects of IT.

IT systems management ensures the reliability, availability, and serviceability of information services and systems. This framework allows a corporation to plan, monitor, and manage enterprise information technology resources in a consistent manner. These resources include people, heterogeneous networks, communications systems, servers, desktops, applications, and databases.

Security Architecture

A security architecture describes the services, mechanisms, and components that reflect the security policy affecting the business functions and technology of an enterprise. The whole notion of protection involves three areas: *security, continuity,* and *control.*

- *Security* — Securing information is guaranteeing its confidentiality (levels of privacy), integrity (being complete and true), and availability (being accessible). The primary purpose of a security architecture is to ensure a common level of understanding and a common basis for design and implementation, by everyone sharing the same resources. Securing these resources is an iterative, cyclical process, involving risk assessment and management, policy, awareness, technology and implementation, security management, and audit functions.
- *Continuity* — Business continuity involves system availability from the perspective of preventing disruption, or having persistence. It has both preventative and reactive components. Failure reduction (preventive) is often as important as recovery (reactive) in a sound business continuity plan.
- *Control* — The security architecture involves languages, document and data structure, processes, data exchange, and control interfaces. It allows an enterprise to express its policy (management desire) and strategy (approach) for security in a coherent manner, to effectively design protected physical facilities and systems of information technology and, in particular, IT infrastructure. Controlled access, which is concerned with the who, how, what, and when of accessing facilities and information, is a major component of security.

Organizational Architecture

This deals with the organizational management of providing business services and products, the management of the services, and IT systems and network management, to include security. This would also encompass all the enterprise management organization capabilities, competencies, role skills, and performance models necessary to implement the desired culture and behaviors.

This architecture consists of three aspects of corporate organization: (1) the assignment of decision rights within the company, (2) the methods of rewarding individuals, and (3) the systems to evaluate the performance of both individuals and business units.

For this text, these definitions are preferred, and they adequately describe the definitions of the basic, logical enterprise architectures. Other definitions will also work quite well, as all but the enterprise business architecture are written about and analyzed quite extensively in many books and texts. This book, however, will adhere exclusively to its own definition of the enterprise business architecture.

Observations and Findings

What do you get when you ask for enterprise models? You get everything from blank stares, to grease boards full of random drawings, to 16-page flowcharts. If you ask, What are the models that you need to represent the enterprise? most likely, you will get blank stares, and sometimes you will get an honest reply of "I don't know." One thing is for certain: there will be no consistency in presentation or in the type of models presented.

The reason that we do not have a generally accepted model of the enterprise with integrated architectures is that we have chosen not to prove its value. If we undertake a serious review of cost overruns, overdue projects, and canceled projects, we will find one of the root causes is a lack of formal, integrated architectures. Essentially, the integrated enterprise architecture is truly unknown. How do we undertake this kind of review? If we initiate the review, we run the risk of embarrassing some senior project managers. Some employees will think we are on a witch-hunt. Others will play the blame game. Fearing these pitfalls, we dodge the review and consequently lose out on building truly integrated architectures.

Integrated enterprise architectures are also a significant *change management* issue within the enterprise. The IT community uses its architectures as a matter of habit, but the business community is not so accepting of using architectural concepts to define the business. The executives have to get on board with the approach and nurture its development and acceptance. They need to educate themselves in its uses and value. It cannot be the COO's or CIO's monthly pet project but the enterprise's project. Its initial development must have exceptional support, enthusiasm, and leadership from the top of the enterprise. The team building the integrated architectures must accept the iterative nature of the process and the difficulty it involves and be encouraged to stick with it.

You can also see in the aforementioned definitions of data/information, application, and network/technology architectures that each builds on one another and refers to one another. Even though each might have a separate author or source, each has the same intent — *integration*. Why then do we not integrate the enterprise business architecture in the same manner? Perhaps it is ownership. It is possible that the IT teams do not feel a responsibility to owning and maintaining the business architecture. After all, it is not IT. Likewise, the business teams do not feel the need to concern themselves with IT because IT exists only to support them.

We have made IT just another function, separating it out for special treatment. Technology is all around us. We wake up to a digital alarm clock, use a microwave to prepare food, drive a car to work, and use air conditioning to cool our offices. Technology is so tightly integrated into our routine activities that it is almost impossible to imagine life without it. That is, of course, until we start thinking about the enterprise. Then somehow IT becomes a separate function.

Because formal business architecture methodologies, techniques, and tools do not really exist today, the business teams feel unsupported. You can find numerous books on IT architectures, but few or none focus on integrated business architectures. The business teams are left with trying to build the business architecture out of the business function/process models, 16-page flowcharts, or, worse yet, the organization chart, and without any formal methodologies to build it anyway. The business community may feel like it is flying an airplane lacking any cockpit instrumentation and with no visible horizon.

Rationale and Justification

Several books reference the enterprise business architecture and its importance to development and evolution of the IT architectures. In *e-Enterprise* by Faisal Hoque,[14] the author states that "by fusing the technology architecture with the business architecture, enterprises can ensure that e-Enterprise applications reflect carefully designed and modeled processes at the same time that they leave the door open to change." With all of this support for fusing and integrating the business architecture with the technology architectures, why have we not formalized a methodology? Perhaps because some business and IT people think that the business architecture does not directly improve profit or it does not reduce costs.

But it does. Could Boeing have delivered the 777 airliner on schedule and under design gross weight without an architecture? No. Boeing was even able to prove that by standardizing the design and architecture of the eight-passenger door latch mechanisms, millions of dollars in savings were possible over the life of the manufacture and operation of the new airliner.[15]

Unfortunately, books describing the "fusing" approach do not exist. Many do not believe it is possible to derive the technology, security, organizational, and human behavioral requirements out of the same business model. But you can with the EBA. Many IT organizations and IT consulting firms do it all the time, just not as formally as defined in this book. Most of the time they succeed in spite of themselves, inefficiently gleaning business requirements out of tomes of textural documents, requiring excessive rework and maintenance down the line. Even when using carefully preserved intellectual capital, these inefficiencies still exist. The only way to survive is to make do or to adopt an approach like the one proposed in this book.

Herein lies one of the best benefits for undertaking this kind of initiative: the architecture teams, both business and IT, will have to work very closely together and in concert. The business teams and the IT teams will have to collaborate and understand one another's architecture better. Each will better realize that they are more than just an individual part, but an integrated component of a unified whole.

Consider that dream home you are building. The dominant architecture is the structural architecture. It must meet the home owner's basic objectives of providing shelter, a certain amount of square footage, and some specific family living areas. It must also provide for car storage, yard equipment storage, phone connections, cable connections, and Internet connections. None of the aforementioned objectives and requirements are achievable without first having a thorough understanding of the structural architecture. You cannot provide an Internet connection unless you know where the walls are and which walls or rooms require the hookups. Do not forget that you also have to connect to the local city's communications infrastructure for Internet connectivity. You may also have to modify the structural architecture to take better advantage of the city's communications infrastructure. Design is the compromise and optimization of conflicting requirements.

For an architecture integration example, consider that the electrical architecture provides the power to heat the home. You also need the walls, beams, and foundation, which support the electrical and heating units. It is impossible to design all these architectures independently and then think that you can integrate them quickly and easily when Tim Allen from the TV show *Home Improvement* arrives in the truck at the empty lot to start construction.

As you can see, all other architectures are based on the dominant structural architecture and analyzed and engineered from a holistic point of view with each other. Each of the architectures is integrated with the others, dependent upon one another, and must provide critical feedback and keen insight as to the design requirements for each. Once you have accomplished the initial integration of the architectures this interconnectivity and interdependency becomes apparent. You then realize that it has no real beginning or end, and that it provides you with a holistic perspective of the enterprise.

Now that we have identified the fundamental enterprise architectures, we need to define the guidelines and requirements for integrating all of them together, holistically. Then we can start building the integrated enterprise architectures. In this book, we will focus on the enterprise business architecture and its development and discuss the foundation it provides in bridging the gap to the other enterprise architectures.

The enterprise architectures exist in your enterprise today and are integrated in some form or fashion, but perhaps hidden from view or in an unknown state. Some are integrated quite formally, and others are held together with "paper clips and chewing gum." There may be several subject matter experts that intuitively understand the various architectures; however, they more than likely do not have formal models representing their composition and touchpoints.

Experience shows that what they have are a mixture of models, some logical, some physical, some in architectural formats, and some in work-flow formats — a patchwork collection at best. Metaphorically speaking, they resemble those junkyard cars built from piles of scrap and other wrecked cars. Little integration is represented between models, and the resulting explanations from the subject matter experts are difficult to comprehend. You just have to trust them that they know what they are talking about without any real empirical data to back it up.

Considerations and Recommendations

All of the integrated enterprise architectures are logical in that each describes what is required and does not describe the physical implementation that achieves the logical requirement. This is the first action that enables the building of adaptive architectures. It forces an understanding of the business and its opportunities and later allows the construction of supporting physical architectures to achieve the desired results without predisposing them to artificial or static restrictions.

The physical implementation then is also viewed in terms of the overall enterprise architecture, holistically, not just based on the interest of the latest hot wireless project. Because we need to consider the enterprise in a constant state of change, the choices for the physical implementation must not only meet the new architectural requirements, but also integrate with the current architectures and have some capability to adapt to the next architectural evolution or the next era. In this day and age, you are never done. You are always evolving and adapting. Stay still, reinforcing the moat around the castle, and you are yesterday's news.

In the closing months of World War II, a B-29 bomber made an emergency landing in eastern Russia. The Russians eventually returned the crew, but refused to return the bomber. They carefully studied the bomber, took it apart, and analyzed its design. It became the architectural model for Russia's first strategic bomber. The same analysis occurred with the engines, but the Russians built a different engine (as a component); however, it still fit within the overall architecture.[16]

Remember the concepts of component architecture. The Russians were keenly interested in the architecture of the strategic bomber. It had value to them, got them into strategic bombing faster, and at a lower cost. Nonetheless, one of the more difficult problems in copying the design architecture was the conversion from English units of measure to metric ones. None of their tool and dye machines were configured for inches, but for centimeters. More recently, let us not forget about the Russian supersonic transport, the Tupolov 144. Of course, the French referred to it as a copied *Concord* or the *Concordski.*

With the four foundational architectures, you can successfully build an integrated enterprise architecture if you understand the interconnectivity and requirements for all of the components. You will, of course, also need to define and develop the components or internal architectures, conforming to the internal rules of integration as well. This is critical to making the architectures operational. It is a challenging undertaking requiring an extreme amount of fortitude, but it is an achievable goal.

Does your enterprise have a generally accepted model that is used and understood by all key employees? Are the architectures integrated, maintained, and analyzed for performance improvements? You may find that you have as many as a dozen models of the enterprise, each used for a different purpose. Perhaps in the near future, industry will form a governing body that will build a standard business architecture methodology or standards similar to what happened with UML and The Object Management Group (OMG).

A STRUCTURE OR SCHEMA

Table 3.4   Need: A Structure or Schema

What do we need?	How do we satisfy the need?
A structure or schema to model the enterprise that allows the integration of each model with the other.	The organizing principle for integration is an enterprise business architecture hierarchy based on *value streams.*

Terms and Definitions

A **schema** is a structured framework that is a codification of rules, constructs, icons, and experience that adheres to a rigorous set of disciplines built around a particular set of semantics and syntax. The schema chosen has to enable the integration of the other architectures and models with the enterprise business architecture.

As previously stated, an **enterprise business architecture** defines the enterprise value streams and their relationships to all external entities and other enterprise value streams and the events that trigger instantiation.

It is a definition of what the enterprise must produce to satisfy its customers, compete in a market, deal with its suppliers, sustain operations, and care for its employees. In addition, the EBA contains the business rules and requirements defined by the business designers and implemented in the value streams.

The EBA is the highest and most dominant architecture — the equivalent to the structural architecture for your dream home. All other enterprise architectures are derived out of the EBA and must be traceable back to the EBA. A similar point of view was expressed by Paul Harmon in his *Business Process Trends* newsletter.[17] Here again, as in your dream home, each architecture requires analysis for optimization from the prospective of the whole enterprise. For all intents and purposes, the EBA is the key "knowledge repository" of the enterprise.

Building the business architecture around a core set of building blocks, or schema, called value streams, is one of the key enablers and precepts to seamlessly integrating the enterprise architectures. The value streams contain the ordered sequence of activities from the functional organizations that produce results. If an activity does not produce a desired result or contribute to a desired result, why does it exist?

Additionally, the metrics and measures for each value stream are tied back to the corporate strategic objectives. This is key to managing the performance of the enterprise. This maintains the required linkage up to the corporate strategy and keeps the whole company focused on the enterprise objectives, not just the functional objectives or the latest hot Web project objectives. Getting thousands of hits on the Web site is not a strategic objective. Gaining higher profit margins out of improved selling chain management is the desired result — the strategic objective. Along the way, you also want to reduce the time it takes to fill an order for a customer, a customer-centric objective, and reduce inventory, a cost reduction objective. This is the potential opportunity strategic e-business planning provides based on analysis of the EBA.

Observations and Findings

Some companies represent their enterprise with a business function/process model, others with a relationship map. Some use numerous multipage workflow charts that supposedly represent the business. It would be safe to say that each case has only a loosely organized set of constructs and icons with little rigor and discipline around semantics and syntax. How then do you communicate across the spectrums of people, processes, and technologies? With any of these examples, how do you possibly evolve, expand, and integrate them with the IT architectures? You cannot with any reasonable effectiveness or efficiency.

After an initial review of the available models on an engagement, most consultants ask for an explanation of how all of the models relate. Here again, they usually get the blank stares or scribbled white board drawings. In most instances, there are only a few people who can explain the models anyway. Needless to say, the models presented to the consultants are not connected or integrated, and are but one perspective of the "elephant." Some clients and fellow consultants state that a fully integrated model is not necessary. If one were to take the models and attempt to integrate them, he or she would fail. Unless you have an underlying structure, one that by design provides direction and discipline, failure is inevitable.

First of all, *none* of the currently popular models were designed with the intent of enterprise integration. Even with all the variations you still cannot do the integration. There are just too many disconnects and leaps of faith. There are no shared concepts, approaches, disciplines, or constructs between the various models. Some people put one of the unrelated types of models up on a wall alongside an IT model and try to explain how the business model led them to the IT model.

This seat-of-the-pants or perhaps "instinctive" approach is predominant in most enterprises today and, surprisingly, sometimes done well by a very senior and experienced systems architect. However, it is doubtful whether the same results are obtainable by another individual provided with the same information. The results are based on the capabilities, keen insight, and experiences of the individual and most likely not repeatable by peers or associates. What is missing is a disciplined approach that allows a team to synergistically develop the integrated architectures and models in harmony and with the necessary detail.

Rationale and Justification

Although any model is an abstraction of some reality, the business architecture is the most tangible representation of reality in business terms. The EBA provides the business rules and requirements for building all other architectures, hence a truly business-driven approach.

The other enterprise architectures in conjunction with the EBA provide an excellent feedback mechanism for additional business improvements and opportunities for building a competitive advantage. For example, consider the numerous business improvements and opportunities provided by the various handheld computing devices, cell phones, and the growth of the Internet. Viewing all of the integrated enterprise architectures holistically and with inherent and designed feedback loops yields synergistic results for the company.

If the organization chart and the business function/process models are both inappropriate as underlying structures, what should be used? If you refer to the definitions of architecture, you will determine that the enterprise blueprint requires an organized set of elements, a principle of composition, and a style and method of design and construction. You can fulfill these requirements with the concept of a value stream as defined by James Martin in *The Great Transition*[18]: "A value stream is an end-to-end collection of activities that creates a result for a 'customer,' who may be the ultimate customer or an internal 'end user' of the 'value stream.' The value stream has a clear goal: to satisfy or to delight the customer."

By decomposing the enterprise into value streams, you get a very effective way of viewing the enterprise holistically. Each value stream focuses on measurement criteria that are important to the customer or internal user. Each value stream is connected to the appropriate external entities as well as other enterprise value streams. The value stream focuses on a result, outcome, or output.

The customer is interested only in the output, not which department or location performed a particular functional activity. With value streams, you get that same focus and alignment, one not duplicated in the organizational chart or business function/process model. It is the value stream's contribution to success in enterprise terms that is measurable (through metrics and measures linked to enterprise strategic objectives); hence, you can reasonably determine its value.

Many executives ask, What is the value of IT? or Can you prove the value of IT? You cannot unless you severely restrict the scope of analysis and confine it to costs only. Then the result of the analysis is very limited. This is analogous to proving the value of accounting, or plant floor scheduling, or inventory management. Which is more important, your heart or your lungs? Or, how about your arms or your legs? This kind of value assessment is meaningless. You need them all, your heart, lungs, arms, and legs, to be effective. They are all valuable. Their true value lies in their integration and ability to work in harmony, not in their individuality. In playing soccer, you need your heart, lungs, arms, and legs to play effectively and efficiently.

In the same vein, to fulfill an order, you need sales, order entry, scheduling, inventory management, manufacturing, distribution, and receivables to deliver the quality product on time to the customer. Trying to determine the isolated value of scheduling or manufacturing in order fulfillment is absurd. By assembling the functional or architectural components of the Order-to-Cash process into a whole, the value stream, you may determine its value, not only to the enterprise, but also, more importantly, to the customer. The value stream concept includes the analysis from the business function/process model and extends it so that all can see the value to the enterprise and customer.

A business case for an Internet initiative or plant expansion initiative must quantify the value of the whole initiative, not just the cost of IT or another department. All value streams affected, all organizations affected, and the customer impact are required for honest analysis. The value comes from the holistic view of the initiative, not from one or two of the more visible or costly parts.

Considerations and Recommendations

In one engagement, it was uncovered that the priority of any initiative was based on the costs of IT. Departmental managers had quickly learned how to "tweak" the numbers to get a higher priority for their project. For example, if the project increased revenue, the business case excluded any budgetary adjustments because the revenue increases were "already in the budget." However, if the project increased costs or needed more people or resources, then the business case requested authorization to exceed the budget because the costs overruns were "not in the budget." The IT estimates were hurriedly provided with requests for "just get me a ballpark estimate." Needless to say, after implementation, the revenues did not materialize, the customers were unaffected, the costs were higher, and IT was frequently behind schedule. What a surprise.

When projects were finally viewed in the context of a value stream based on a sound business case, a far better assessment of priorities was possible. Another added benefit was a happier customer, along with a more predictable schedule, more accurate cost estimates, and attainable revenue increases. With this approach, you can link the initiatives back to the measurable objectives found in the corporate strategy. You begin to sequence the initiatives based on their contributions to the enterprise priorities, not by how a department manger tweaked the IT numbers.

Once the activity's effectiveness is determined, its efficiency is analyzed next. Opportunities for improvement abound during the effectiveness and efficiency analysis. Choices for discontinuing the activity or moving it to the Web are available for analysis, not in a stand-alone fashion, but in the context of the whole enterprise. Options for reusability surface as well as redundancies are identified, and other improvements emerge.

With an inspired and motivated team, out-of-the-box thinking will flourish and breakthrough initiatives will evolve. This is achieved by viewing the enterprise holistically, through an understanding of its architectures — an achievement unmatched if viewed through the functional organizations without the integrated enterprise architectures.

What underlying, integrating structure do you use for your enterprise? Do you use the organization chart, business function/process model, or a relationship map? Is the structure well known and understood? Does it provide a foundation for integration with the other architectures and corporate strategy?

A COMMON LANGUAGE

Table 3.5 Need: A Common Language

What do we need?	How do we satisfy the need?
A common language, one that spans the enterprise and is comprehensible from the top to the bottom of the organization chart, that is understandable regardless of which organization, department, or division you are assigned.	The communications medium for creating a shared understanding between people, processes, and technologies requires a *common modeling language* rich in constructs that can describe the enterprise's framework of models in precise and clear terms.

Terms and Definitions

An enterprise is a complex entity. To model complex entities in precise and clear terms and to a significant degree of detail, you need a rich, modeling language and, because you have a very important story to tell, one that can be readily understood by many. Why do we want to build a model of something as complex as an enterprise and restrict the builder to a handful of outdated constructs that lack constructive nuances? We need a rich, *common modeling language* to share and articulate our understanding of the enterprise to the widest audience possible.

For example, try to describe your latest vacation, ski holiday, scuba diving trip, or family reunion. Think about all the exciting and wonderful things that happened and what became some of your most enduring memories. Now, prepare to describe it but with one stipulation: avoid the use of colorful descriptive terms, adjectives, adverbs, hand gestures, and facial expressions. Bet you cannot do it. If you can, it is probably boring and inaccurate.

The use of a common language for modeling, decomposing, and integrating architectures is required. A more graphical and richer modeling language is preferred. Do not seek the lowest common denominator when considering modeling languages. A rich modeling language enables better communication through more precise graphical representations. It also forces the team members to listen and communicate better because each has to communicate through a modeling language that should allow him or her to articulate everything that needs to be said. This learning and use of a rich modeling language actually enable better communication. Instead of listening to just words, arguments, and opinions, each team member seeks to understand the ideas and concepts represented by the common language in the models.

The models provide the communication medium for creating a shared understanding between people, processes, and technologies. Really good models stand alone and do not require detailed explanations as to what is illustrated. Two people's review of the model must result in a common and shared interpretation. It is perfectly acceptable to ask why some process was designed in a particular way or why the illustrated process is underperforming. Better the "why" than "what" is the model trying to convey.

The common language, through the syntax and semantics of its constructs, is the key enabler for integrating and deriving the architectures. It also provides the common language through which sales, ordering, manufacturing, distribution, IT, and all other departments can communicate and consequently integrate.

Enterprise Business Architecture — Modeling Language (EBA-ML) (copyright © 2004)[19] is a rich and comprehensive modeling language for the business architecture. The syntax and semantics of the EBA-ML constructs clearly and precisely communicate business rules and system requirements. It enables you to portray the enterprise value streams from a fully integrated or holistic perspective. It also connects to crafted object-oriented software development, packaged software configuration, IT architecture development, or process simulation software. Today these connections are empirical rather than systematic, but the basic discipline for connecting to other IT domains is sound.

Observations and Findings

A review of existing models during the early days of an engagement usually finds several disturbing things. The most prevalent: one team cannot read and understand another team's models without a fairly comprehensive presentation. This is because none of the models are consistent in presentation, style, or format. Very few models contain graphical representations for inputs and outputs, as this is usually found only in the supporting text. In addition, most often the models are out of date with no plans to make them current.

On one engagement during an internal model review, it was observed that a reasonable adherence to flowchart symbols was followed. Numerous multipage flowcharts were presented. The consistency was fairly good throughout all of the division's models except for one detail that stood out. On numerous models, additional symbols with limited consistency were annotated. The reason for this was the modelers felt the need to express something graphically, but because no approved symbol was appropriate, they created some. There were so many that you almost needed a cross-reference of ad hoc symbols to fully understand the models. If your notation does not contain enough graphical symbols to communicate the process's purpose and objective, why are you using it? How can you tell a colorful story about your once-in-a-lifetime vacation without colorful, descriptive terms, adjectives, adverbs, facial expressions, and hand gestures? You cannot, and the same applies to an enterprise model with a limited set of authorized symbols or constructs.

There are just over 30 EBA-ML constructs, each with a well-defined syntax and semantics. The shapes of the constructs also provide insight into their purpose and meaning. However, there are those who for various reasons just do not want to conform to an existing business modeling language. These people prefer to reinvent the shapes and change the syntax and semantics. We believe that a month later, they will still be changing the icons. When they finally finish, they will have duplicated most of the EBA-ML constructs, but with different shapes and some differences in syntax and semantics. Other than the time they have wasted, they are right back at the starting point of choosing a business modeling language.

The authors have used various modeling languages since 1995. For the models developed in this book, refer to Appendix A for the semantics and syntax of EBA-ML's constructs and use it just as you would a dictionary. For example, when you need to understand a construct in a model, look at how the construct is used and then refer to the appendix. Avoid just getting a hard and fast definition from the appendix and then looking for a place to use the construct. Always use the notation in the context of the EBA models. The last page of the appendix contains a quick-reference summary of the constructs.

As you probably already know, UML has risen to prominence as an object-oriented modeling language and is complemented with RUP. Just refer to *UML Distilled,* second edition by Martin Fowler and Kendall Scott[20] and *The Rational Unified Process* by Philippe Kruchten,[21] respectively. EBA-ML is a rich modeling language geared toward business design, but it still integrates with any object-oriented software development modeling language and process, including UML and RUP. It neither conflicts with nor duplicates anything in UML/RUP. It simply allows the evolution of the business workflow models or, if you prefer, the business use cases to object-oriented software development.

By effectively using the integration aspects naturally inherent in the EBA, the transition from business to IT is more precise, accurate, and feasible. You have an opportunity to reduce the number of omitted specifications and develop requirements more clearly. You can minimize the translation and restatement from the business design phase to the technical design phase. Hence, you improve the efficiency of the software development process.

On one occasion, an object-oriented programmer/analyst questioned the validity of this point of view. He was somewhat skeptical about the transition from a business modeling language to UML. In addressing this issue, there are two points to consider:

1. If he was somehow able to read volumes of textural requirements documents and figure out the objects, their classes, the activity diagrams, the sequence diagrams, the collaboration diagrams, and the state transition diagrams, then he could certainly figure out the same from the graphical representation in a workflow format. But instead of parsing nouns and verbs from volumes of textural requirements looking for objects and methods, would it not be easier to analyze a business use case modeled in a rich modeling language and skip the tedious and error-prone parsing? This parsing technique as described by Iseult White in *Using the Booch Method*[22] creates a lot of "noise."

2. He just tried it and was quite pleased with the results. The programmer/analyst later stated that he might have to participate in the workflow development for two reasons. The first reason was to ensure that the workflow models were capable of evolving into UML artifacts. The second reason was to provide some insight during the requirements analysis phase that might take advantage of current and maturing technologies. He felt that this contribution might result in increased customer satisfaction, higher degrees of automation, and other process improvements. The business guy and the IT guy are now collaborating and working in harmony to build a competitive advantage for the enterprise.

Rationale and Justification

Along with the rich modeling language, you need a set of rules on how to employ the language. For example, this book was written in the English language, using the generally accepted rules of English grammar. It would not have made sense had the English language been used with the rules of Japanese grammar. It just will not work. Similarly, to develop systems using object-oriented code, one uses UML as the language and RUP for the rules or processes. Here we use EBA-ML as the language and the EBA approach for the rules or processes. The EBA processes are illustrated later in the case study.

Let us consider the concept of a common language of the business architecture for a moment. UML has evolved over the past several years as the predominant object-oriented modeling language. How do we connect the business architecture with the various IT architectures? How do we derive the IT models out of the business models? The constructs of the business architecture not only need to describe the business, but also need to empirically translate to the first iteration of UML. This provides the common language between the business designer and the IT designer. Eugene McSheffery's white paper[23] describes a very similar approach for using business process models in the flowchart format to get to UML.

As the concepts and constructs of a business architecture common language evolve and mature, this translation will also evolve systematically, ultimately allowing the development of software that translates the business model into an IT model. A similar event occurred years ago when data models were first utilized as manual input to code generators. Then, for example, James Martin developed information engineering (IE), and later software tools were developed that automated most of the translation.

These early computer-aided software engineering (CASE) tools were not universally accepted; however, they moved the IT industry out of the dark ages of unstructured programming. Whether the same will happen between the business architectures and IT architectures is anybody's guess, but the concepts and principles are sound. It is the vision of the designers that will make this work.

Not only must the business architecture connect to UML, but it also must connect to the first iteration of any packaged software configuration, for example, an enterprise resource planning (ERP) package or a financial package. Once the business designer and IT designer have communicated through the business architecture, the IT designer may continue further development into any other IT domain applying other acceptable methodologies, approaches, techniques, and tools to transition from the logical models to the physical implementations. However, this connection is not a one-time event, but an iterative one. Numerous opportunities for business improvement will surface from development of the IT architectures, models, and software artifacts. This feedback loop from the IT architectures to the business architectures results in continued creativity and additional process improvement ideas.

On another project, the architecture, workflow, and event models were used to link to the initial configuration of an ERP software package. Unfortunately, almost two months of poorly controlled and poorly structured modeling efforts resulted in the development of numerous workflows using the old flowchart notation. It had previously been agreed upon to build the enterprise business architecture, the whole, from the functional workflow models, the parts. In other words, build the core cross-function processes, such as Order-to-Cash, from the functional components, such as Web order entry, credit checking, scheduling, manufacturing, and distribution.

The result was disastrous. The initial review looked like a hanger full of the debris from a crashed airplane. Nothing fit together and nothing flowed from one function to another. Obviously, integrated business architecture thinking was absent. The models only presented the view from a functional perspective and had nothing to do with the customer's perspective. To make matters worse, the flowchart notation was not applied consistently and it too had many ad hoc symbols created by the various modelers.

It was believed by management that it was too late to change the notation, but acceptable to tweak and standardize the symbols. We first used a rich modeling language as a guide to match up the most frequently used symbols with those of the flowchart notation. In essence, we used a subset of its constructs to match the flowchart's symbols. This was certainly not a perfect solution, but an acceptable one given the circumstances.

Next, it was necessary to enforce the discipline of adding inputs and outputs to the models. If a functional activity produced output A, and another functional activity used A as input, then both models had to consistently conform to the notation standards and text description. Both models had to illustrate A as the output and input, respectively. If one activity called it A and the other B, but it was intended as the same thing, then the two modelers had to reconcile their naming differences.

Once the flowchart standards were adopted and the inputs/outputs reconciled, we were able to build the business architecture using combined modeling teams consisting of business designers and ERP analysts. By using the value stream concept to build the core cross-function processes, we were able to put an integrated high-level business architecture together. Obviously, the intent was to build an effective model that was capable of linking to the ERP configuration. And it worked. We had a reasonably good, shared understanding of how the enabling IT was to support the business design. Lesson learned: adopting a common notation at the beginning would have avoided a lot of rework and effort.

Considerations and Recommendations

There are more than a few obvious problems with using the flowchart notation. One problem is that it is widely used with a lot of variation in the symbols or constructs. Unless you have someone strictly monitor the model development and the use of the symbols, you will get some variation in the communication and understanding of the models. Remember, you want a shared understanding out of the models without a lot of discussion and persuasion on what they represent. In a model review session, you want people asking, Why did you design the business process that way? and not What is this model trying to communicate or produce? You want to spend time discussing improvements to the business design, not wasting time explaining the model to the reviewers.

Of course, you may use supporting text with any graphical representation when appropriate. It is extremely difficult to model intuitive thinking and instinctive behavior. For example, how do you model a customer service representative handling an irate customer? You may find it more appropriate not only to describe some relevant approaches in text format, but also to provide some examples as well. Here again, do what makes sense and use a text format and the graphical representation in a complementary fashion.

A second problem with the flowchart notations is the overuse of the line with an arrowhead. Between activities (or boxes), it represents "flow of control," and between an activity and a data store, it represents an "output/input." In some interpretations of a model, a reviewer might think that the "flow of control" is to a data store. More experienced reviewers might better understand the intent, but why have it subject to interpretation? You need separate constructs for "flow of control" and "creation of outputs." A rich modeling language should clearly differentiate between "flow of control" and "creation."

A third problem with the flowchart notation is again with the overuse of the line with an arrowhead for identifying inputs and outputs. When drawn from an activity pointed to a data store, it is an output. When drawn from a data store pointed to an activity, it is an input. How then do you represent an update or change? Some use a double-headed arrow between the activity and data store. In EBA-ML, you have six distinctive constructs to represent the most frequently used relationships between activities and inputs/outputs: "create," "retrieve," "update," "delete," "receive or consume," and "constraint or rule."

A fourth problem with the flowchart notation is that it poorly illustrates concurrent or simultaneous processing. In today's business world, you have to shorten the critical path in the process. One possible solution is concurrent processing. There are no constructs available in the flowchart notation for this representation, although some tools provide a set of parallel bars in some flowchart templates, which represents concurrent processing. In software development, when using UML activity diagrams, you can easily illustrate concurrent processing with the "fork" and "join" constructs. In EBA-ML, you use a set of parallel lines, which contain multiple workflows for concurrent processing.

Let us revisit that new CEO reviewing the enterprise models. If they are modeled properly with a rich modeling language, the new CEO will not require all of those presentations from the various C-level executives. Once the modeling language is learned, the models will serve as the communications medium, providing clear, concise, and accurate information. The new CEO and the existing C-level executives will have a common ground from which to communicate. The "what" the enterprise "produces" is presented in the models, and in some of the lower-level models, a little bit of the "how" is described. Because the models start out at a high level, the new CEO can choose the appropriate level of detail to seek understanding. The new CEO may move all around the model, up and down at will.

Hopefully, several "why" questions will develop, which will also give the new CEO some keen understanding and insight into the design of the enterprise business architecture. The same opportunities will exist for a new middle manager, someone transferring between organizations, or a new employee. Here again, the focus is on the results and outcomes, not just the tasks performed.

Is there a standard modeling notation used by your enterprise? Does the notation create a shared understanding between business and IT teams?

A WAY TO UNDERSTAND COMPLEXITY

Table 3.6   Need: A Way to Understand Complexity

What do we need?	How do we satisfy the need?
To understand a complex enterprise, to break it apart for analysis and improvement, and then put it back together again, better than it was before and without breaking everything else.	To analyze complex enterprises, apply the *basic principles of decomposition* around both processes and data.

Terms and Definitions

Decomposition is the art and science of the separation of an entity into constituent parts or elements or into simpler compounds in such a manner as to allow reconstruction back into the original entity or whole.

We need to decompose the enterprise just as we decompose an airplane for construction or maintenance. The enterprise, like an airplane, is just too complex and complicated for a single one-page display or view with all of its detail. Decomposition enables analysis and improvement of components with an understanding of the impact to the whole. For example, you can understand the decomposition of an airplane using its bill of materials (BOM) and an architectural diagram to understand how all of the parts fit together to form a whole.

A **bill of processes (BOP)** is to an enterprise as the BOM is to an airplane. In a similar manner, it allows you to understand the decomposition of the enterprise and to understand how all of the parts fit together to form a whole.

Along with a BOP, which conceptually provides the same information as the BOM, we need an enterprise decomposition schema and approach for both processes and data. This begins the evolution toward a component architecture.

A **component architecture** is one that ensures that all of the parts for a particular entity fit together properly. Conceptually, we need a component architecture for an enterprise, that is, one that allows all of the activities, inputs, and outputs of the enterprise to fit together by design.

For the **enterprise process decomposition** approach of the EBA, consider the following definitions and refer to Figure 3.5:

- *Enterprise entity model*: The enterprise entity represents the highest-level model of the enterprise. It illustrates the relationships between all external entities such as its customers, suppliers, stakeholders, service providers, regulatory agencies, and infrastructure providers. It identifies all external inputs and outputs with their respective sources and destinations. It decomposes into a single enterprise aggregate model.

- *Enterprise aggregate model*: The enterprise aggregate represents the first level of decomposition. It illustrates the relationships between all group aggregate models and it identifies all external inputs and outputs with their respective sources and destinations. The enterprise aggregate decomposes into the group aggregate models.

- *Group aggregate model*: A group aggregate represents the encapsulation or consolidation of some group of value streams for some specific purpose. For example, you may choose to group all customer-related value streams into a group called "customer centric" or all employee-related value streams into a group call "people caring." The value streams are the building blocks of the group aggregate models. Usually three to six group aggregate models exist for the typical enterprise. The group aggregates decompose into value stream architecture models.

- *Value stream architecture model*: The value stream architecture defines the workflows or business use cases. It encapsulates or consolidates the various enterprise workflows into organized business use cases. Anywhere from 16 to 24 models exist for most enterprises. Multiple levels of this architecture model may exist, but there must be at least one level. All of the business use cases have at least one event, which activates or instantiates the designated workflow or business use case. Refer to the events illustrated in the value stream event model. The value stream architecture model decomposes into the workflow models.
- *Workflow model*: The workflows illustrate the sequence of activities and actions necessary to transform the inputs into the required outputs for each business use case. A workflow is activated by a business event. It is from the workflows that one transitions to lower-level models for decomposition or to specify requirements in text. These workflows (and activity) models are the business-driven requirements that are used as input to crafted software development or vendor product configuration. Here again, there may be multiple levels of workflow. The highest or first level of workflow is the business use case model. The lower-level models down to the last level of workflow are called activity models.
- *Activity model*: The activities illustrate the most elementary and basic collaboration between humans, between humans and computers, and between computers. Sometimes the models are referred to as the "swim lane" models. The collaborating entities are noted in horizontal (or vertical) "swim lanes," which illustrate the flow of control between activities performed by each entity. These models are also the business-driven requirements that are used as input to crafted software development or vendor product configuration. It is possible to link this model to the activity diagram and sequence diagram models found in UML. This is the last and final model in decomposition.
- *Peer model*: Models that provide an alternate view of interest at the same level are peer models. There are only two standard peer models: the value stream event model and the value stream environment model. For display purposes, the value stream event model should be placed and viewed to the left of the value stream architecture model, and the value stream environment model is viewed to the right of the value stream architecture model.
- *Value stream event model*: The value stream events show the initiating external and internal events that trigger or invoke a workflow instance in a value stream architecture model. The events trigger, activate, or instantiate a business use case. An event is something that happens outside an enterprise (external) or business area (internal to the

Enterprise Hierarchy Model with Descriptions

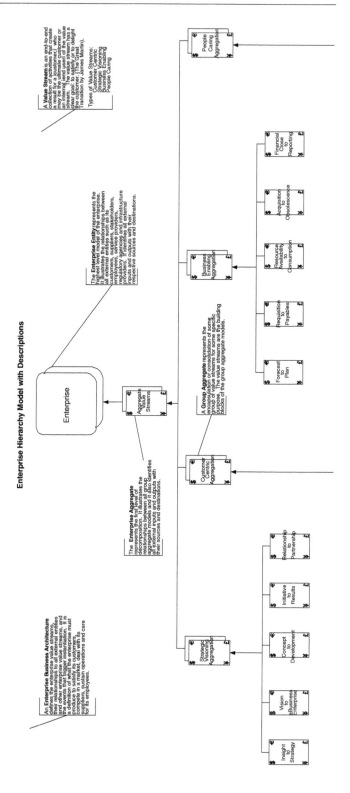

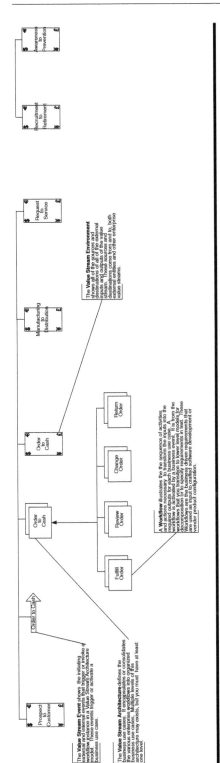

Figure 3.5 Enterprise Hierarchy Model with Descriptions

enterprise), to which the enterprise must react in a preplanned way (a business response). An external business event is caused by an external entity. An internal event is caused by another enterprise business process. A temporal event is caused by the passage of time. Build the value stream event model at the same level as, and in sync with, the value stream architecture model. If desirable, aggregate these event models into an enterprise event model.

■ *Value stream environment model*: The value stream environments show all of the sources and destinations of all of the external inputs and outputs of the value stream. These sources and destinations refer to both external entities and other enterprise value streams. Most of the model's information is simply repeated from the higher-level group aggregate model. You may also use the value stream environments to show something of special interest. Consider using this model for presentation purposes or as the value stream source of information to create presentations.

For the **enterprise data decomposition** approach, consider the following: All external inputs and outputs of a process are described in the models. Some are simple and elementary, while others are aggregated. There are three types of aggregated data: *shared properties, containers,* and *whole/parts.* Each decomposes into lower-level elements, or if you prefer, the individual elements are aggregated into a higher-level grouping. Within each type of aggregation, other types of aggregations, both similar and different, may exist. For example, a shared property element may decompose into other shared properties, which again may decompose into other containers or whole/parts.

The aggregated or decomposed information about inputs and outputs should be maintained in a **lexicon** directory; for example, see Figure 3.6. By referencing items in the lexicon directory, we can represent information at a higher level without all of its supporting detail. Here again, it allows us to represent something complex, but simply. All inputs and outputs are found in the lexicon directory. The three types of aggregated data are defined as follows:

■ *Shared properties*: A shared property element shares a set of relationships or common characteristics between aggregations of elements. Elements are anything in any combination, such as airplanes, cars, or PCs, or anything else we can identify. An element can be a "kind of" or "type of" another element. This is the case when they share properties. For example, the element aircraft may decompose into two elements — jet aircraft and propeller aircraft. Both are types of aircraft that share some properties, but also have

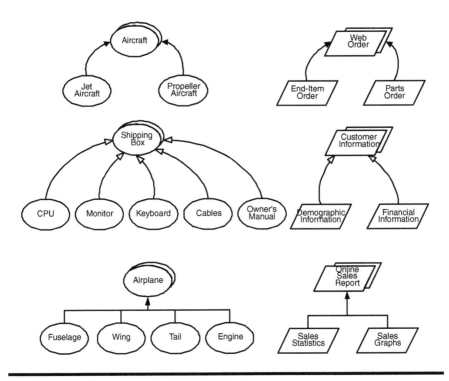

Figure 3.6 Aggregated and Decomposed Information

something unique that differentiates them from each other. This is a simple description that avoids the need to separately describe each element.

■ *Containers*: A container represents a collection of elements for a specific purpose. For example, a shipping box contains a CPU, monitor, keyboard, cables, and owner's manual. Here again, a container is a simple description that avoids the need to separately describe each element.

■ *Whole/parts*: A whole/parts element illustrates the relationship between various parts that when integrated or connected, form a whole. The whole is greater than the sum of its parts. For example, an airplane is composed of a fuselage, wing, tail, and engine. Without the wing or engine, you do not have an airplane, but rather a static display. Here again, a whole/part is a simple description that avoids the need to separately describe each part.

For keeping the process decomposition and data composition in synchronization, consider the following: All external inputs and outputs in a higher-level (parent) model require representation in a lower-level (child) model. The two levels of models are then defined as in balance.[24] All external inputs and outputs are connected to their sources and destinations from the enterprise entity model down through the value stream environment model. The value stream architectural models and other workflow models do not require these external source and destination connections. Continuing to illustrate the sources and destinations gets too cumbersome the farther down you get in the decomposition. Describing the sources and destinations in a workflow model may also lead to confusion with regard to flow of control. These sources and destinations are more appropriately represented in architectures that do not illustrate flow of control.

For balance checking between levels (enterprise entity, enterprise aggregate, group aggregate, value stream architecture, value stream environment, workflow, and activity), verify that all external inputs and outputs on the higher-level models are represented on the decomposed lower-level models. The verification includes the text description and the construct of the input or output.

Observations and Findings

The Boeing 777 airplane has over three million parts. Talk about complexity. What about the complexity of the newest aircraft carrier, the USS *Ronald Reagan*? A Boeing 777 airplane, as well as an aircraft carrier, has a huge and complex bill of materials. Over 10,000 people, grouped in 238 teams, representing 14 countries, participated in the design and manufacture of the Boeing 777 airplane.[25] Yet the first Boeing 777 airplane was delivered on schedule and under design gross weight. How is it possible to build these complex and huge objects and have them work as designed?

Obviously, architecture is of paramount importance. You just cannot start building an airplane or aircraft carrier from the front, back, or somewhere in the middle. You have to view the airplane as a whole and then carefully partition the airplane into components, and the components into subcomponents, and the subcomponents into sub-sub-components, and so on. You have to use the art and science of decomposition.

We need the same kind of rigor and discipline around the architecture and decomposition of the enterprise. Instead of a bill of materials, conceptually, we need a bill of processes. The airplane has a component architecture, one that ensures all the parts fit together properly. Here again, conceptually, we need the same kind of component architecture for the enterprise, one that allows all of the activities of the enterprise to fit together. You can assemble the airplane, put it into service, disassemble it for routine maintenance, replace parts as necessary, or even install redesigned parts, reassemble it, and put it back into service. What you cannot do is saw it into numerous pieces and expect to reassemble the chunks back into an aircraft that will fly safely.

However, some managers think that this "sawing behavior" is acceptable for an enterprise. How many times have we seen a new corporate reorganization "saw" the enterprise into pieces? Then several months later, the enterprise goes through another reorganization or "sawing" evolution. It is a wonder that anything still works after a few reorganizations. Nonetheless, the enterprise seems to eventually recover, healing the "sawing" wounds just as the body heals an injury — an advantage an enterprise has with its people over the airplane with its mechanical parts.

In presentations given by clients about their enterprise, they usually present a few slides on the corporate organization, including locations and divisions. Except for the organizational chart view, none of the presentations decompose the enterprise the same way. Descriptions about the integration of one part with another are limited and usually very high level. Sometimes it is doubtful if the interworkings of the various organizations are understood by the presenter. If asked any kind of detailed question, the presenter usually refers to someone else. If asked, What happened after the last reorganization? there is no lack of detail here, just all kinds of colorful and interesting stories and several insights as to why so many problems occurred.

Rationale and Justification

The component architecture of the enterprise with its BOP must operate just as the component architecture of the airplane with its BOM. This concept expands the focus of the enterprise away from just the functional departments or organizations to include value streams. You might cling to the functional organization chart and claim that you can build the same capability. However, for each occurrence or instantiation of an activity, you will have to assemble several functional activities "on the fly." To do this assembly, you have to have a plan and the plan will ultimately turn into a value stream. This on-the-fly assembly creates numerous inefficiencies, rework, waste, and frustrated participants. So why not start with the value stream concept to begin with?

A part for an airplane has some sort of attaching or connecting mechanism, such as a cable, bolt, rivet, coupling, pipe, hose, or electrical circuit. For it to fit properly with another component, each must share the same connectivity specifications. To expect this connectivity to occur at assembly without a proper design is ludicrous. However, we expect this magical connectivity to occur in the enterprise immediately after an enterprise reorganization. Here again, we get away with this corporate behavior because of the healing capabilities of the dedicated teams of people in the enterprise. This healing behavior is basically nothing more than damage control.

Conceptually, for the enterprise the connectivity is maintained with the architecture through the inputs and outputs of each process. Instead of a cable, bolt, or hose, there is an invoice, Web order, electronic funds transfer (EFT), or physical receipt of goods. Here is where the discipline and rigor of adhering to an architecture becomes important. The specifications for the inputs and outputs must have the same exactness as those for a cable, bolt, rivet, coupling, pipe, hose, or electrical circuit if the expected results are to be attained.

Decomposition of the enterprise is required to manage complexity. Proper decomposition with value streams around inputs and outputs, or results, reduces the complexity of the enterprise into manageable and integrated elements. It also enables the possibility of outsourcing with well-defined requirements and business rules for each activity or component. This first step enables an evolution of the enterprise away from functions and toward a component-based architecture.

The enterprise decomposition evolves around an output or result for a customer (or supplier), not an activity or function. As previously noted, the best way to decompose an airplane is according to its BOM. You never decompose a whole entity by carving it into a random collection of pieces. The same is true for an enterprise. Value streams enable you to decompose the enterprise into its BOP in a cohesive manner.

The value streams are also the building blocks of higher-level value systems such as customer relationship management (CRM) and supply chain management (SCM). This is where you architect the CRM or SCM solution, rather than cobble it together from the functional organizations and departments.

Enterprise decomposition requires a schema for both processes and data. For processes we start with a high-level enterprise model and decompose it down to the lowest-level activity model. For data we start with carefully grouped or classified aggregations of data and decompose them down to their most elementary items. In some instances, you may choose to start with lower levels of processes or data and aggregate them up. This is generally much harder, less efficient, and involves a lot more balancing and leveling support.

Nonetheless, some people prefer to start where they are comfortable and knowledgeable. They start with their workflows and then work up through the aggregations. In practice, you will work in all directions: top to bottom, bottom to top, middle to top, and middle to bottom. The ultimate result is usually the same as long as you keep the process and data decomposition synchronized with the generally accepted rules of balancing and leveling.

When it comes time to reorganize the company, use the value streams instead of the organization chart as the starting point. It is certainly all right to consider the organization chart; just do not use it as the primary source. Focus the reorganization around the outputs produced, not the activities performed by the various departments. View it as an assembly of well-connected parts, to create a whole, not as a sorting mechanism for placing parts in a warehouse bin.

How well does the concept of a BOP and enterprise decomposition scale? Does it work for a $100 million company as well as for a $100 billion company? You can decompose a small single-engine airplane according to its BOM, just as you can the Boeing 777. However, the 777 will take a lot more hanger space, time, and energy. And, of course, the same holds true for a sailboat versus an aircraft carrier. No matter the size or complexity of the entity, it just takes adherence to the required rigor and discipline of decomposition with the rules of balancing between higher and lower levels of architecture. The same applies to a small enterprise or a large one. It will just take more time and energy for a large enterprise.

Once the value streams are identified and initially connected through inputs and outputs, you may start concurrent analysis, decomposition, and BOP development of the other value streams, down through their lower levels. You treat each value stream as a component, in a similar way as you design the components of an airplane. For example, when you discover the need for another input from another value stream, you must make the corresponding update and communicate with the providing value stream and vice versa.

Considerations and Recommendations

Through the aforementioned decomposition of the enterprise, we can build a component architecture starting with the business rules and requirements. Several efforts are afoot today to build this component architecture, but up from the IT perspective. It is far more difficult to build up from the bottom than to architect down from the top. However, ultimately, the same result may develop — a set of component building blocks capable of assembly through configuration into a complete whole.

Most companies use the organizational chart as the principle of construction. Perhaps the business function/process and organizational chart models may provide some additional insights, but it is doubtful either will provide the glue to hold everything together. Just as in the airplane each part's connectivity with a cable, bolt, rivet, coupling, pipe, hose, or electrical circuit is required, in a similar fashion the business architecture requires each component's connectivity to an input or output. The descriptions for an invoice, Web order, EFT, or physical receipt of goods require the same exacting specifications as for the parts of an airplane.

Regardless of which approach is taken, you will ultimately have to assemble the components into operational value streams. If you try to build a model based on the business functions/processes — what is done, as opposed to what is produced — you will lack the integration and connectivity inherently present in the value streams.

How is an enterprise decomposed today? Do peer managers understand the decomposition of each other's processes and how each is integrated with the other? How will your enterprise respond to decomposition around value streams and away from organizational charts? You may find some welcome relief with the value stream approach. Some managers say that they had intuitively made the integration connections, but were unable to formally articulate them in a formal fashion. Here again, the lack of formal methodologies inhibits your progress.

ENTERPRISE PRIORITIES

Table 3.7   Need: Enterprise Priorities

What do we need?	How do we satisfy the need?
To prioritize and promptly implement those strategic initiatives that produce predictable and measurable results in the best interest of the enterprise.	An *enterprise strategy* with its strategic initiative road map provides insight and direction based on the return on investment.

Terms and Definitions

Strategic business planning is the process of defining the mission and long-range objectives for conducting the business and developing the strategies for achieving them.[26]

Enterprise architecture planning is the process of defining architectures for the use of information in support of the business, and the plan for implementing those architectures.[27]

In **strategic business planning**, envisioning the new and evolving enterprise is very demanding and requires committed, dedicated, and insightful executive leadership. This leadership team needs the current (as is) enterprise architecture as input into developing the future (to be) enterprise architecture. These architectures are not dangling loose somewhere in the enterprise, but directly related to the enterprise strategy and critical to the supporting initiatives. Both the current and future enterprise architectures are necessary to build the transition plan for evolving from the current to the future enterprise architecture. The transition plan contains the strategic initiative road map, essentially the design of the corporate DNA.

Observations and Findings

If you review the priority initiatives of a typical enterprise, most likely you will get an excellent series of presentations. Each initiative will have some well-defined measures of success and a business case for justification. However, in many cases you will get a very weak explanation of how the initiative contributes and supports the enterprise strategy. You can also ask a manager that is one level higher or lower in the organization chart and get a different answer. In a few rare cases, you might get the response of "I don't know."

Also, ask about recently completed initiatives. Did the initiative meet or exceed the expectations of the enterprise? What were the metrics and measures that determine a successful initiative? How did the customer respond to the initiative? Unfortunately, there is very little proof of success. It seems the key measures of success are how close the initiative came to meeting its estimated budget and its implementation date. Although these are certainly important, what about the return on investment? If the initiative was expected to generate an increase in new customers and a decrease in lost customers, how did it perform? If the initiative was expected to reduce the product delivery time from a week to three days, did this happen? If delivery time was reduced as expected, what happened to inventory levels? Did the volume of Web orders increase as predicted, or did you just get more Web hits and inquiries? These are the types of questions that should be answered to measure success.

In some cases, metrics and measures are used in a punitive fashion or to blame other departments and teams for problems. This behavior is characteristic of immature, ill-informed, and insecure management organizations founded on political relationships. These managers are just "dancing bears" out to make themselves look good, sometimes at the expense of their peers. We need to refocus this energy toward the customer and growth for the enterprise. We do not want one initiative competing with another, but through a cooperative spirit, supporting one another.

We have to maintain a fierce alignment with the strategy and keep track of the numbers religiously. Without this record keeping, we do not have a feedback mechanism. We need for this feedback mechanism to close the loop in the value stream. This is the regulating effect that helps us tweak and tune the processes in the value stream. Without this information, we are just guessing. After all, implementing a corporate initiative is not a spectator event, but rather one that involves commitment from leadership, and really a commitment from everyone.

Rationale and Justification

Strategic business, IT, and enterprise planning require frequent updates based on the changing nature of the markets served and the business strategy. Here are some of the questions that need answering for strategic planning:

- How do customers view our enterprise?
- How does our enterprise achieve its corporate objectives?
- How do the stakeholders view our enterprise?
- How do suppliers view our enterprise?
- How do we enable and support our enterprise?
- How do our employees view our enterprise?

To find these answers in legacy-based function/process thinking, you must cobble together in an ad hoc fashion several functional organizations and departments, sometimes called a cross-functional process. If you are researching a customer complaint or material shortage problem, you may find one department blaming another rather than working together to resolve the problem. It is also very difficult to measure performance or link the results of a particular organization back to the enterprise strategic objectives. Getting thousands of hits on the Web may delight the Web master and provide some interesting bits of information for the IT infrastructure support group, but what you really need is thousands of Web orders in sales as predicted out of a strategic initiative. In a nonintegrated environment, an enterprise reorganization requires a new, ad hoc approach every time and you start all over again just as imprecisely.

Just about any strategic enterprise initiative requires a thorough understanding of the integrated enterprise architectures. New product development, e-business design, plant expansion, mergers, acquisitions, business continuity planning, and disaster recovery all require a keen understanding of the EBA for development. Additionally, each needs an awareness and understanding of the other initiatives for proper sequencing of implementation and leveraging of resources.

Just about every company has a vision, mission, goals, and objectives. However, the real manifestation of that vision is not found posted on the walls in the lobby of the corporate offices or cafeterias, but in the daily actions of the leaders and employees of the company. If the vision is real and compelling, you will see evidence of it every day in the leaders and employees through results. Hardwired to the vision are the strategy and corporate objectives with their supporting metrics and measures.

Additionally, the enterprise initiatives should have well-defined expectations for accomplishing results and positively influencing the metrics and measures of the corporate objectives. This meeting or exceeding of the corporate objectives then enables the achievement of the vision. You then refresh the vision, corporate objectives, and enterprise initiatives and do it all over again. Just staying put or resting on your laurels gives the competition a chance to catch up or, worse, take the lead.

Some strategic engagements identify excellent initiatives with an assigned set of priorities. Now the tough part begins. How does an organization design, implement, and support the initiative, and along the way meet or exceed its measurable results and expectations? How do you contribute to the initiative and champion its purpose?

This is accomplished by aligning the results and contributions of the enterprise value streams with the strategic initiative's measurable goals and objectives. Of course, some of these measurable goals and objectives will have a direct association with the customers. Those initiatives that make the highest contributions are implemented ahead of those that make lesser contributions.

If your department or organization feels left out of the game, then use the creativity and insight of your team to find an appropriate strategic initiative that gets you back in the game. Now, instead of following a political agenda, you are following a corporate agenda. Many important initiatives have developed outside a formal strategic engagement. It is this kind of creative thinking, working in harmony with a strategic engagement, that leads to breakthrough results.

The enterprise initiatives most likely are evolving or changing the architectures of the enterprise. In some cases, the initiatives are engineering new architectures (developing new capabilities) and, in other cases, reengineering existing architectures (enhancing existing capabilities). Some of the initiatives are collaborative in nature, such as building an SCM capability off an ERP backbone. During the implementation of these initiatives, their effectiveness and efficiency are greatly influenced by the leaders' understanding of the architectures. Well-understood enterprise architectures that are properly integrated enable implementation of the aligned initiatives, usually within budget and on schedule. This level of maturity and sophistication often meets or exceeds the corporate objectives, thereby achieving the vision. It sounds simple, but it is not.

Quite often, corporate initiatives fail to complete or achieve the expected results, especially if they require a lot of supporting IT. The reasons for this are numerous. Some run out of funding, the corporate priorities change, or the initiative champions move on to other things.

The foundations of these problems are found in unaligned, out-of-sequence, and unfocused initiatives, most likely using unstructured architectures. Hard wiring the vision, objectives, initiatives, and architectures is the best preventive to failure, but not a panacea for all problems.

Now that everyone understands the linkage from the corporate vision through the enterprise initiatives, you can start engineering the enterprise. You build a strategic initiative road map, assigning the priority of initiatives based on their contributions to improving the corporate objectives, which when met achieve the vision. In some cases, an initiative may require understanding or documenting the current architecture and designing the future architecture. This enables development of a transition plan for the initiative, which of course includes the resources, budget, and schedule.

This holistic view of the enterprise from the perspective of the customers, suppliers, stakeholders, employees, and competition is critical to implementation of the initiatives. The road map provides direction, and the holistic view, through its understanding and keen insight, provides the will to execute the initiatives.

Considerations and Recommendations

Initiatives do not stand alone, even when aligned with the strategy. They may complement other initiatives and synergistically influence one another. The sequencing of initiatives may also optimize the expected results and leverage the investment. An amusing TV advertisement shows the employees of a new dot.com company watching the first Web orders growing faster than expected. Their excitement and enthusiasm quickly turn into anxiety as they realize that they cannot respond to the demand. Perhaps their strategy should have considered how to expand their production and supply chain capacities along with a rapidly expanding customer base. They may have focused on just one or two initiatives, such as facilitating ordering, but not understanding the impact on the rest of the enterprise. This simple example illustrates the paramount need for a sound strategy — one that is truly focused on the future of the whole enterprise, and not just on the function of Web ordering. The strategy must have objectives, which when met, achieve the vision defined in the strategy.

How does one align the objectives? To base the alignment on the functional organization is extremely difficult and usually hard to track. Using well-defined values streams in the EBA as the basis for alignment provides you with a way to lead and direct any visionary or improvement initiative. Remember, the value stream has a focus on the customer (or internal customer). Measuring the impact on the customer is extremely important to the enterprise. Enterprises that continue to succeed have this kind of strategic focus. Some enterprises develop into world-class corporations with this kind of thinking. However, none of these world-class corporations achieved success because of a focus on some independent, unaligned, functional initiative. Rather, the opposite occurred. They understood how to lead and direct the enterprise from a holistic view, and not a view of just the more critical functional departments.

Does your enterprise have a strategy? Is it operational, evolving, and periodically updated to reflect opportunities and changes in the marketplace? Are you aligning the initiatives with the strategy, using the metrics and measures as guidance?

THE CUSTOMER VIEW

Table 3.8   Need: The Customer View

What do we need?	How do we satisfy the need?
A customer-centric view of the enterprise, one that puts the customer first and foremost.	The enterprise must first measure its success from *the customer's point of view.*

Terms and Definitions

A **customer-centric view** is one that focuses on the perception that the customer has of an enterprise. A customer rarely views the enterprise in terms of a single department, but rather as the product or service that is delivered and paid for.

Value streams enable and support a customer-centric view of the enterprise. After all, by definition, the **value stream** has a clear goal: to satisfy or to delight the customer.[28] The focus of the value stream is its outputs, products, services, results, and outcomes. You measure the results and effects through a proper feedback mechanism, tweak and adjust, and start another cycle all over again. Here you get the synergy of a customer-centric focus implemented through the value stream concept for the whole enterprise. Through causality relationships identified in the EBA, you understand how a value stream contributes to enterprise success and how it impacts other value streams.

Observations and Findings

We need to stay focused, especially on the customer. However, we also need a balanced view of the enterprise, including its people, partners, suppliers, and regulatory agencies.

By building an enterprise business architecture using the value stream approach, we will in effect align all core processes (and most activities) with the enterprise's true value-creating system: its customers. Many companies have a value stream or core process called "order fulfillment." This point is discussed in *Reengineering the Corporation* by Hammer and Champy.[29] This value stream, sometimes called a core process, is an excellent example of focusing on the customer. Sometimes the value stream has an executive as its owner or, as suggested by Hammer and Champy, a process owner.[30] By using the value streams and understanding their inputs and outputs, we can better analyze the contributions of the various supporting departments and organizations.

It is mandatory and critical here to see the value stream as the customer sees it. Some exceptions to this point may arise when dealing with customer service, but you will not find an unhappy customer just blaming the billing department or marketing department. Unhappy customers will hold the entire enterprise accountable, and they are not usually very forgiving if their problem is compounded by poor customer service. When customers walk away, they leave the whole enterprise, not just the billing department.

The integration of the architectures and the alignment to the vision are conceptually easy to develop but most difficult to implement. What makes it difficult is overcoming the politics of the functional organizations and departments. Getting them to think holistically and putting the enterprise first is a very difficult task. Most people forget the customer and hold their allegiance and loyalty to their functional boss, assuming that their boss has the best interests of the enterprise in mind.

Herein lies the first opportunity for integrating the enterprise architectures and communicating the value of the EBA. You get the entire company to understand the whole enterprise and how the enterprise initiatives link to the corporate objectives, which in turn link to the vision. Once this is done, everybody is properly aligned and focused on what is important to the enterprise and can see how their contributions impact the vision and the customers.

An anecdote told by J. Carlzon in *Moments of Truth*[31] describes two stonecutters hewing square blocks of granite out of a mountain. Each was asked to describe their contributions. One sadly replied, "I am cutting this mountain into square blocks." The other smiled and proudly responded, "I am building a cathedral." Obviously, the first stonecutter's view of the enterprise was a simple description of a routinely performed functional activity. The second stonecutter's view was a holistic understanding of the vision of the enterprise with a focus on results and customers, not just activities.

Consultants frequently ask their clients to describe their view of the enterprise. Invariably, they get a very detailed description of the organization chart and numerous colorful and insightful stories about the corporate history. Along the way, they get some descriptions of products and services and some of the new initiatives to enhance these and develop new ones. Then toward the end, maybe the clients throw in something about the customer, usually couched in the current buzzwords of the day.

What happens when you ask, What products and services does your customer want next? In most cases, you will get weak and shallow answers, usually because middle managers are not involved in product development and just do not know. As for the higher-up executives, you get some excellent discussion on what is happening with current products and services over the next four to six months, but very little about what is happening in the next two years. Perhaps there is a concern here for intellectual property and confidential strategic plans; however, the focus is usually tactical, with limited emphasis on the customer.

Rationale and Justification

There are several ways to view the enterprise:

- One view is centered on the functional organizations and the corporate organizational chart. If you want to know the focus of your enterprise, just review some recent executive presentations on current and future activities of the enterprise. If you have a new executive coming on board, you may sense a corporate restructuring on the near horizon. What is the purpose of the restructuring? Usually the rationale is to better serve the customer, but is this the truth behind the reorganization?

   In one company, the last time a new executive came on board the restructuring was cost based. What was hard to understand was how the prior organizational structure was inherently creating higher costs. No one could figure out how the prior organizational design was allowing cost to get out of hand. Even worse, no one could understand how the new organizational structure was, by design, going to inherently contain or reduce costs. The new executive expected everyone to accept the new reorganization on faith and that it would improve simply because the new executive said so. But why did the former executive build the enterprise with these inherent problems? As you might suspect, after the corporate restructuring, a new round of layoffs occurred and the enterprise was saved, cost was under control, and all was well, that is, until the next meeting with Wall Street.

■ A second view is centered on the products and services produced by the enterprise. In several cases, these products and services are built on a foundation of core competencies. You can look over the last 10 to 15 years at leading companies with dominance in their respective fields. Where are they today? Some still dominate their marketplace, but many have fallen from grace.

Several people were amused and amazed at the mid-1980s paradigm shift from host compute management to distributed compute management. One senior IT executive stated that all of that wasted and idle compute power sitting on the desktop was going to kill the potential of the PC. However, the executive forgot to ask the PC user how he might like to use it. However, Apple did, and so did Microsoft, as well as a lot of other start-up visionary companies; consequently, a new market exploded on the scene. The core competency of managing host compute was slow to evolve to one of managing the awesome power of distributed computing. And then along came a new executive with a brand new restructuring plan to refocus on expanding the distributed computing business model.

■ A third view is centered on the customers served by the enterprise. In some cases, you also see the key suppliers mentioned as partners in serving the customers. In *21st Century Jet*,[32] a senior Boeing executive was describing the company's customers to a group of employees in a team meeting. He said that the customers wanted an airplane bigger than the Boeing 767 but smaller than the Boeing 747. He knew this because he had asked them and listened to them. He also acknowledged that pleasing the customers is really tough. Nonetheless, Boeing went on to develop the new 777 commercial aircraft.

Boeing was again confronted with a similar dilemma. Should it build an airplane bigger than the 747, which the French decided to build, or focus on the sonic cruiser? The French Airbus A380 is a huge, double-decked 555-passenger airliner. With a new wing and fuselage design,[33] the sonic cruiser, about the size of the 250-seat 767, is almost one hundred miles per hour faster than the existing fleets of subsonic airliners. This choice is a tough one. In some instances, the customers, in this case the international air carriers, are asking for both. However, if the international air carriers ask their flying customers, what kind of response will they receive? Many of the flying customers will most likely prefer getting there sooner rather than later in the company of 555 other passengers.

Considerations and Recommendations

Let us hope that you are seeing executive presentations describing your market opportunities and customers, not your organizational structure, and not just the latest enhancements to your existing products and services. The customer-centric view of the enterprise is the one each of us needs to have. We certainly need a balanced exposure to the other views, but we must have a concentrated focus on the customer. You effectively and efficiently achieve this using value streams.

It is doubtful if any really effective customer type measures are possible from a purely organizational chart view. There are several functional metrics and measures that are important to the various departments. It is just that in some cases, functional goals come into conflict with enterprise goals and, consequently, customer satisfaction.

For example, one client's advertising department rushed to get a promotion mailed with the monthly statements. The only problem was that they forgot to tell the service center about the launch of the promotion. The service center representatives were caught totally unaware of the new promotion. The promotion was ultimately successful, and the advertising department launched the promotion on schedule, but the service center had to scramble to get on board. Do you think a fully defined and integrated value stream could prevent these kinds of problems in the future? As we have said before, through causality relationships identified in the EBA, you can now understand how a value stream contributes to enterprise success and how it impacts other value streams.

Do you view your enterprise from the organizational view, products and services view, or the customer-centric view?

SPANNING LIFE CYCLES

Table 3.9   Need: To Span All Life-Cycle Phases

What do we need?	*How do we satisfy the need?*
To span all life-cycle phases from planning through operations, enabling the transition from the current to the future state.	Any enterprise initiative must consider the iterative nature of business cycles, integrating people, processes, and technologies from *strategy to results.*

Terms and Definitions

The **domain of the enterprise** consists of its *people, processes,* and *technologies.* Any strategic initiative supporting the enterprise must address all three and span the **continuum** from planning, through design, through implementation, and eventually through operations. It must also provide for the transition from the current (as is) state to the future (to be) state. The continuum is illustrated in Figure 3.7.

A single, universally accepted, industrial-strength **strategy-to-results** methodology addressing all facets of the enterprise does not exist today. However, the solution is achievable under the umbrella of a framework that encompasses the integration of several approaches, methods, and tools, recognizing that it is necessary to include the embedded base of processes, models, and technologies that already exist in the enterprise. The critical aspect here is to find those complementary approaches, methods, and tools and integrate them effectively and consistently.

Figure 3.7 also illustrates another critical aspect, which is the overlap of approaches, methods, and tools within the continuum. In *Business Engineering with Object Technology,* David Taylor[34] defines **convergent engineering** as business design implemented directly in software with an absolute minimum of translation or restatement. Here again, the balanced and leveled external inputs and outputs in an EBA minimize this translation, thereby enabling the convergence of the architecture, workflow, and event models from planning through operations.

Additionally, this approach satisfies the need to integrate from strategy to results. That is, from the workflow models, which describe the numerous enterprise processes and activities, you transition from the business domain into the IT domain with the minimum of translations and restatements. Gleaning the IT requirements out of a functional textual document, even if it is a use case, requires an unnecessary amount of subjective interpretation. Transitioning from a graphical business model built with the same formal discipline as found in the development of the UML models is possible using this integrated enterprise architecture approach. Even if you are configuring packaged software, the same holds true, as the workflow models represent the logical requirements of the business, independent of the physical implementation.

From the holistic perspective, we can build the EBA, which serves as the mother of all architectures and contains all of the enterprise value streams. These value streams, by design, are tied to the strategy, vision, and corporate objectives through the various metrics and measures that determine success. From the workflows or business use cases found in the value streams, one develops the first iteration of the UML models or the initial configuration of the packaged software — hence, fulfilling the

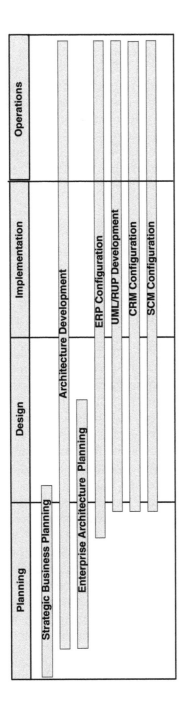

Figure 3.7   The Life-Cycle Continuum

needs of the business continuum from strategy to results and minimizing the translations and restatements noted above.

For those of us who frequently travel to different locations for consulting engagements, we sometimes ask for directions to the client's office or airport. No one can provide us with clear directions unless they know where we are currently located. You have to know the current location to direct someone to a future location. The same is true if you are about to implement, for example, a CRM package or a business intelligence package. You need the current state (as is) as well as the future state (to be) defined before you start. Then you can build an appropriate transition plan, or set of directions, for achieving the desired results, spanning the continuum from strategy to results.

Observations and Findings

On most engagements, you will get a brief review of the small stuff. If you ask what are the priorities based on, you will usually get a multitude of answers. Surprisingly, to the client, a large percentage of IT spending is not linked to the corporate strategy. Here we are, at the end of the strategy-to-results continuum, and we are spending significant IT dollars on orphan-type projects.

You find similar results with the big stuff. Additionally, you find breakdowns among major life-cycle phases, sometimes caused by management pressure to get a phase signed off that is behind schedule. Experience shows that the impact of this behavior is more rework and problems in the later development and implementation phases. This almost always happens when you just throw it over the wall to keep moving.

One might say that "the buck stops in construction and coding." After all, if it is not coded, you cannot just sign it off and send it to testing if it does not exist. Coding and testing highlight design flaws, expose gaps in requirements, and bring clarity to business requirements. In the early project life-cycle phases you can get away with poor specifications and sketchy requirements because there is no real way to formally test the completeness and continuity of the textural documents. But if you have modeled the enterprise properly, it is harder to get away with this behavior.

We must also leverage the current investment and embedded base in the enterprise. It is usually easier to start something new and build from a clean slate than it is to expand and integrate from what already exists. Therefore, the real opportunity for synergy lies not only in integration, but also in reuse. The result is a common set of integrated enterprise architectures and models that decompose down into the new and existing embedded base of models. The approach described in this text spans all life-cycle phases from strategy to results and provides an integrating capability with existing methods and tools.

Of course, some extensive rationalization and reconciliation are necessary to fully integrate the enterprise. This integration then provides you with the ability to effectively manage a heterogeneous technology environment, to bind the multiplicity of technologies within the enterprise, and to understand and communicate the relationships among processes, applications, information, infrastructure, and other management frameworks. Without the integrating and linking capability of the integrated enterprise architectures and models, a new approach, method, or tool obviates the predecessors, creates another "dangling participle effect," and stimulates more debate or competition on choice of approaches. Obviously, the enterprise needs a solution, not a debate.

Usually, priorities for the small and big stuff are based on some kind of informal steering committee's recommendations and available budget, and not on the corporate strategy or awareness of the EBA. If the IT budget is based on functional allocations, the belief is that the functional departments will wisely spend the money. After all, these were hard-fought-for dollars during the last annual budgeting cycle and were somewhat based on what was spent last fiscal year and partially determined by projects that crossed the fiscal year boundary. There is very little, if any, return on investment for some of these projects — just costs.

Managers can provide you with the associated cost information almost immediately, but it will take them a few days to come up with any formal return-on-investment numbers. Many will also have trouble linking it back to the strategy. If you want to stir the pot in the next budget cycle, use a zero-based budget approach. Present all major and minor projects, both new and those in flight, with their link to the strategy and a business case based on contributions to the enterprise. In doing so, the next budget battle might yield better results for the enterprise.

The inability to span all life-cycle phases from planning through operations and the inability to rationalize and reconcile the business through the use of integrated enterprise architectures, as described above, highlight the lack of any continuity from strategy to results as well the strategic alignment issues to be found in the normal enterprise. The large percentage of IT spending not linked to the strategy is symptomatic of the lack of a strategy-to-results approach. If a sound and operational strategy-to-results approach exists, then the number of orphaned projects are inherently reduced. Instead of focusing on the orphan projects and placing more stringent controls on their priorities, back up to the strategy and fix the problem at the source. Along the way, provide a structured approach for linking strategy to results in a continuum.

Rationale and Justification

The integrated architecture approach provides ways to link the strategy to design and ultimately the strategy to the operation of the initiatives and projects. In addition, the transition from logical to physical or from one domain to another is supported. As time goes on, the "to be" models get richer in detail and cover more enterprise processes. Most likely, it is impractical to stop everything and build a comprehensive set of "as is" integrated architectures and models. It is far more practical to build them as you go, from the implementation of one initiative to another. This keeps you linked to the strategy, integrated from strategy to results, and reduces the costs associated with the orphan projects.

In today's environment sans the EBA, we typically have several initiatives under way that do not support any enterprise strategy. Additionally, we do not transition from one major project phase to another with formal design artifacts. Initially, the major functional specifications are written along with the supporting requirements from other functional areas. Regardless of the level of participation from the supporting functional areas, requirements are omitted because the impact of a new specification is unknown. This usually occurs because no formal model or formal knowledge repository exists to document all of the touchpoints with all other functional areas. The requirements and specifications gathering participants can only rely on their inherent knowledge and experience and some informal peer reviews. It is unrealistic to take a tome of only functional specifications, throw it over the wall to the IT functional teams, and expect results delivered on time and on budget.

With the integrated enterprise architectures and workflows, you are not throwing it over the wall, but rather are clearly and precisely transitioning from business design to technical design and doing so in an iterative fashion. The artifacts produced are known and understood by each design group with a more complete and comprehensive set of specifications. The transition from business design to UML/RUP or to packaged software is more predictable and formal. Therefore, it is fair to expect fewer disruptions to the project's schedule due to fewer omissions of touchpoint type requirements and better-described specifications. Once we are aligned with the enterprise strategy, we can advance the project from the planning phase to the design phase to the implementation phase and, finally, to the operations phase.

The integrated enterprise architecture approach analyzes the sequence of projects and adapts to future methodologies and technologies. It accomplishes this by connecting to and reusing the embedded base and by remaining logical, not physical. The physical implementation is described in the lower-level models for both current and future business requirements.

As you can see, you are logical early in the life cycle and physical later in the life cycle.

For example, in the logical business architecture, you may see a technology output (the *what*) to a supplier. However, you will not know whether it was created via an electronic data interchange (EDI) or Web transaction running on a UNIX- or NT-based platform (the *how*). Nor will you know if it was created instantly or transmitted once every hour (the *when*). These physical details are described in the lower-level models and in the domain of the previously selected methodology and technology. The logical business architecture simply provides the vinculum, or the binding and integration capability shared between initiatives, to all of the varied domains, both future and current.

When using a fully integrated business architecture with well-defined workflows, your analysis of these business rules, requirements, and specifications will help you determine your choices for implementation. If you choose to implement a packaged software solution, you may have to reconcile and transition from your workflows to the workflows defined in the packaged software to synchronize the packaged software processes with your desired processes.

Hopefully along the way you will also discover some IT and process improvement capabilities inherent in the packaged software. Here you need to rationalize and reconcile the differences in the two workflows to optimize the performance expectations. You can exploit the capabilities of the packaged software while you customize it for your particular needs. This not only gets you optimized performance, but a more predictable project plan and budget. The objective is optimized performance for the enterprise, not an adaptation of the packaged software to fit the "as is" model. Unfortunately, this behavior was the norm in Y2K projects.

If you choose to develop the software, the transition to UML uses the very same models and architectures as packaged software. Your transition point to UML or packaged software may occur at different levels in the model, but nonetheless with the same model. By having the business and IT analysts collaborate on the business design requirements, you have another opportunity to optimize the performance expectations. The IT analysts may offer some very creative alternatives to manual processes with some of the emerging capabilities of new technologies. Here again, the objective is optimized performance for the enterprise, achieved through the synergy of the business and IT analysts' collaboration. This behavior may create the nexus to success for the initiative.

In many cases, legacy systems are built without any formal methodologies or models. A suggestion here is to use the newly developed detailed business architecture and workflows because they will provide better rules, requirements, and specifications than any textural document.

However, you may choose to transition from the workflows to text at a certain level in the model to better integrate with the legacy systems and their supporting approaches. This makes perfect sense and keeps the alignment with the strategy and the adherence to the strategy-to-results concept.

Considerations and Recommendations

If you do not believe the points previously made about strategy to results, ask one of your senior project managers or senior program managers to present his approach to you. If he cannot present it to you within a couple of hours, maybe the formalities of his approach really do not exist. See if he can start with the strategy and take you all the way down to the results, tracing the requirements along the way and explaining the relationships. If he requires a few days to put it together, then this is a probable indication that a formal approach may not exist at all.

Usually, a manager's initial response is to assign a single project manager and core team for the duration of the project. The intent of this is to provide some continuity from one project phase to another. This is an excellent technique. Now think of the possibilities of using the integrated enterprise architecture technique with the core team — we have the synergy of the two techniques complementing one another. As we build the depth and breadth of the integrated enterprise architectures from one initiative to another, we develop a repeatable process with ever-increasing levels of predictability and a repository of reusable intellectual capital. By staying focused on the strategy, we are implementing those initiatives that have the greatest impact on the whole enterprise.

The key to this kind of thinking is obviously the integrated enterprise architectures. It is in harmony with the Zachman Framework[35] and does not conflict with the UML/RUP methodology, CASE methodology, packaged software methodology, or some other life-cycle methodology. The architectures and models better integrate the strategy-to-results phases, in many cases substituting graphical models for text, richer and more accurate in greater levels of specificity. It does not exclude textural specifications, but shifts the emphasis from text to more graphical models.

What is the percentage of text and models in the specifications today? By far the most frequent answer is 90 to 95 percent text. With the integrated enterprise architectures, your first initiative may achieve a 60/40 percent text-to-model ratio. This is an excellent start and you are well on your way to reversing the trend. You have realized that this is no different from building your dream home. Those architectural diagrams are used consistently throughout the building of your dream home. Perhaps you and the architect have made a few changes along the way, but can you even imagine trying to build a home with only textural descriptions and no architectural diagrams? To have an effective and efficient strategy-to-results approach requires the same formal architectures and models that building your dream home does.

From the corporate strategy, let us assume that you have several major initiatives. Each of these initiatives is integrated with and sequenced with the other initiatives. Each initiative has multiple projects, some IT only, some process only, and some both. Here again, each project is integrated with and sequenced with the other projects. And of course you may have some projects in one initiative sequenced with other projects in a different initiative. At the beginning of the analysis is the "as is" business model and architecture of the enterprise. To represent the future state of the enterprise we have a "to be" business model and architecture. As previously noted, these models are logical at the higher levels, independent of the physical implementation choices.

Is your strategy-to-results approach formal or more of a throw-it-over-the-wall type? Are your initiatives sequenced for optimization?

OTHER BASIC NEEDS

The eight needs are summarized above, as well as the rationale behind them explained and how to satisfy the needs discussed. However, that does not mean that these are all of the needs that you must satisfy. For example, you need exemplary leadership and a dedicated commitment for this kind of undertaking. You need adequate funding and the perseverance to see it through. It is assumed that the reader accepts this point of view and will therefore allow further discussion on satisfying the eight needs mentioned above.

REFERENCES

1. *IEEE Standard Glossary of Software Engineering Terminology*, 610.12-1990 (Washington, DC: IEEE, 1990).
2. Steven H. Spewak and Steven C. Hill, *Enterprise Architecture Planning: Developing a Blueprint for Data, Applications and Technology* (Wellesley, MA: QED Publishing Group, 1993), 1.
3. Francois B. Vernadat, *Enterprise Modeling and Integration: Principles and Applications* (New York: Chapman & Hall, 1996), 31–32.
4. Christopher Koch, "IBM's New Hook," *CIO* magazine, July 1, 2003, http://www.cio.com/archive/070103/index.html.
5. Philippe Kruchten, *The Rational Unified Process: An Introduction* (Reading, MA: Addison-Wesley Longman, 1999), 101.
6. James Martin, *The Great Transition: Using the Seven Disciplines of Enterprise Engineering to Align People, Technology, and Strategy* (New York: American Management Association, 1995), 104.

7. Vernadat, *Enterprise Modeling and Integration*, 32.
8. Chris Marshall, *Enterprise Modeling with UML: Designing Successful Software through Business Analysis* (Reading, MA: Addison-Wesley Longman, 2000), vii.
9. Kruchten, *The Rational Unified Process*, 100.
10. Vernadat, *Enterprise Modeling and Integration*, 156.
11. Spewak and Hill, *Enterprise Architecture Planning*, 169.
12. Harjinder S. Gill and Prakash C. Rao, *The Official Client/Server Computing Guide to Data Warehousing: The How-To Guide for Implementing Your Own Data Warehouse* (New York: Macmillan Computer Publishing, 1996).
13. Spewak and Hill, *Enterprise Architecture Planning*, 223.
14. Faisal Hoque, *e-Enterprise: Business Models, Architecture, and Components* (Cambridge: Cambridge University Press, 2000), 18 (foreword by Tom Trainer, introduction by Dale Kutnick).
15. *21st Century Jet*, KCTS Seattle and Channel 4 London, Copyright © 1993, Channel 4 London.
16. Von Hardesty, "Made in the U.S.S.R.," *Air and Space Smithsonian*, February/March 2001.
17. Paul Harmon, "Business Process Architecture and the Process-Centric Company," *Business Process Trends* newsletter, March 2003, http://bptrends.com.
18. Martin, *The Great Transition*, 104.
19. Enterprise Business Architecture — Modeling Language (EBA-ML), Copyright © 2004, Ralph Whittle, Plano, TX.
20. Martin Fowler with Kendall Scott, *UML Distilled: A Brief Guide to the Standard Object Modeling Language*, 2nd edition (Reading, MA: Addison-Wesley Longman, Inc., 2000) (foreword by Grady Booch, Ivar Jacobson, and James Rumbaugh).
21. Kruchten, *The Rational Unified Process*.
22. Iseult White, *Using the Booch Method: A Rational Approach* (Menlo Park, CA: Benjamin Cummings Publishing Company, 1994), 30.
23. Eugene McSheffrey, "Integrating Business Process Models with UML Systems Models," 2001, http://www.popkin.com.
24. Tom Demarco, *Structured Analysis and System Specification* (Englewood Cliffs, NJ: Prentice Hall, 1979), 341 (foreword by P.J. Plauger).
25. *21st Century Jet*.
26. Spewak and Hill, *Enterprise Architecture Planning*, 86.
27. Ibid., 1.
28. James Martin, *The Great Transition*, 104.
29. Michael Hammer and James Champy, *Reengineering the Corporation: A Manifesto for Business Revolution* (New York: Harper Business, 1993), 118–119.
30. Ibid., 102.
31. Jan Carlzon, *Moments of Truth* (New York: Harper Collins Publisher, 1989) (foreword by Tom Peters).
32. *21st Century Jet*.
33. Bill Sweetman, "Plane Fast," *Popular Science*, July 2001.
34. David Taylor, *Business Engineering with Object Technology* (New York: John Wiley & Sons, 1995), 10–11.
35. John A. Zachman, *The Zachman Framework*, http://www.zifa.com.

4

PUTTING IT ALL TOGETHER

A DIFFERENT WAY OF THINKING

Before we put all of this together, we need to understand a few things. We are going to have to think differently about the enterprise and, at the same time, not forget what we already know and have learned about the enterprise. This is not an *or* argument or a choice between new and old ways of thinking. It is not this approach *or* that approach *or* some other approach. This is an *and* approach, a collaborative approach that adds a new dimension to our way of thinking.

We are going to expand and build on what we already know and find ways to exploit our existing knowledge and views of the enterprise. We do not need to fuel debates about approaches, methodologies, techniques, and tools. However, we do need to find ways to synergistically focus our energies on building a value-creating system for the enterprise. We want our competitors to internally debate how and why they are losing market share and profit.

Here is a rather abstract example of thinking differently. Imagine that you are a two-dimensional being living on a flat plane and that you are unaware of three-dimensional objects.[1] Then one day you observe a weird phenomenon in your normally simple two-dimensional world. You notice the appearance of a very small dot on your plane that suddenly begins to expand. Although frightened, you cannot resist the urge to observe this phenomenon. The dot continues to expand in a circular fashion and then begins to shrink in a circular fashion until it returns back to a dot and then disappears. Others of your kind have also witnessed the phenomenon, but no one can seem to explain it. Perhaps your fear and anxiety grow. You may begin to describe this phenomenon as a new force in your universe or perhaps as a deity. It defies all known laws in your flat, two-dimensional universe.

As time goes on, you learn to live with this new phenomenon or force of nature. Then you experience an epiphany. In seeking to understand this phenomenon, you begin to expand your thinking about the observations of the expanding and shrinking circle. Suddenly, you hypothesize the concept of a three-dimensional object called a sphere. You were able to do this by expanding your thinking about the geometry of a circle and all of its mathematical properties. After much analysis and study, your new concept is accepted and understood by all.

A sphere, passing through a plane, will suddenly appear as a dot, begin expanding as a circle, later shrink back to a dot, and finally disappear completely. You are now able to explain and understand the phenomenon, having expanded your thinking from just two dimensions to three dimensions. All of the laws of plane geometry still apply; however, you have expanded your thinking to another dimension. The only thing you lost or abandoned was an assumption or restriction on your thinking. The phenomenon never changed, but your thinking expanded to conceive of new possibilities. You could even say that you experienced a paradigm shift.[2] What was initially inconceivable and feared is now understood and simply explained.

This is always an entertaining activity in the opening presentation of an enterprise business architecture (EBA) engagement. Now ask each participant to describe his or her current role in the enterprise in some detail. Then ask, "What do you produce?" Think about how you might respond to these questions in the presence of your manager or customer. During the role discussions, most respond with "I am on the Web team" or "I am an executive manager in operations" or "I am a systems analyst" — all with colorful details and descriptions. Sometimes we have to cut them off to keep the discussion moving. However, during the "What do you produce?" discussions, the answers are very brief and sometimes followed with dirty looks and cold stares.

On one occasion, a manager humbly responded, "I don't think I produce anything." Well, we had fun with that one, but the very next participant responded with a bowed head and mumbled, "I produce problems." We could not believe these responses, especially in a joint meeting with the client and outsourced information technology (IT) participants.

Once the laughing stopped, we just had to ask about the "I produce problems" response. The participant described his network teams' responsibilities and customer expectations, detailing the numerous problems with keeping the network up and stable. The impact on the customer was obviously impacting productivity. Not only was the participant's answer honest and candid, but the answer had taken the customer's view of the services produced. The team was producing problems and not producing a stable, efficient, and operational network.

As awkward as this may seem, this is what we want. We want everybody to first think in terms of what they produce, *not* what they do or where he or she is on the organization chart. This is the added dimension we must have to view the enterprise holistically. We need the open, honest, and candid understanding of our products and services as viewed by the customer without blaming individuals or organizations. This is the starting point to building a value-creating system for the enterprise.

WHAT DO YOU PRODUCE?

The following excerpt from a book titled *Out of Control* by Kevin Kelly[3] provides a good example for analysis:

> *Levi Strauss*, makers of jeans for the whole world, has networked a large portion of its being. Continuous data flows from its headquarters, its 39 production plants and its thousands of retailers into a economic super-organism. As stonewashed jeans are bought in the mall in, say, Buffalo, a message announcing those sales flies that night from the mall's cash register into *Levi's* net. The net consolidates the transaction with transactions for 3,500 other retail stores and within hours triggers the order for more stone-washed jeans for a factory in Belgium, or more dye from Germany, or more denim cloth from the cotton mills in North Carolina. The same signal spurs the networked factory into action. Here bundles of cloth arrive from the mill decked in bar codes.
>
> As the stacks of cloth become pants, their bar-coded identity will be followed with hand-held laser readers, from fabric to trucker to store shelf. A reply is sent back to the mall store saying the restocking pants are on their way. And they will be, in a matter of days.

What does Levi Strauss produce? Obviously, the answer is jeans and a variety of clothing items and accessories for around 3,500 retail stores. We understand this quite easily, but Levi Strauss also produces other things in the process, for example, purchase orders for dye, cloth, and other needed raw materials. We can actually take this high-level description of Levi Strauss and, using the EBA insight, start to build a graphical model.

For the purposes of analysis, the following example will use a fictitious company called *The Only Denim Jeans Factory*. This allows the discussion to address topics that better illustrate and explain the EBA approach without using a real company. After all, this discussion is about the EBA, and the fictitious company is just an example.

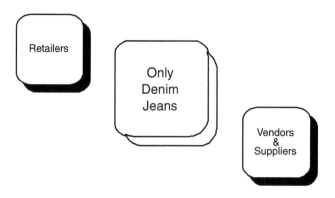

Figure 4.1   Only Denim Jeans and External Entities

We will initially represent The Only Denim Jeans Factory in the center of our model using the Enterprise Business Architecture — Modeling Language (EBA-ML) **entity** construct. All discussion will center on The Only Denim Jeans Factory as the reference point. We will also represent all external enterprises with the EBA-ML entity construct, but smaller, with a darkened edge. Additionally, we will keep the example as simple as possible, referring only to the high-level model. This will allow an easy introduction to the use of EBA-ML. Refer to Figure 4.1.

We also need to represent the inputs and outputs and their relationships between The Only Denim Jeans Factory and its retailers and suppliers. In this simple example, the inputs and outputs that are physical in nature are represented by the EBA-ML **aggregated physical input/output** construct. The creation of jeans for the retailers and the receipt of raw materials from the suppliers are physical in nature. Those that are technology related are represented by the EBA-ML **aggregated technology input/output** construct. The order for jeans, purchase order, customer payment, and vendor payment are technology related. They are all aggregated because there are several kinds of each with shared properties. For example, the jeans come in different styles, sizes, and colors. Referring to Figure 4.1 for the relationships between the enterprise and its inputs and outputs, we will use the EBA-ML **create, retrieve, and receive or consume** constructs. When The Only Denim Jeans Factory produces an output, the create construct is appropriate. When The Only Denim Jeans Factory receives data from a technology source, the retrieve construct is appropriate. When The Only Denim Jeans Factory receives a physical input, the receive or consume construct is used. Refer to Figure 4.2 to see the EBA-ML constructs that we will use.

We will begin development of the model by starting with the creation of orders for jeans from all of the retailers each night. We represent this

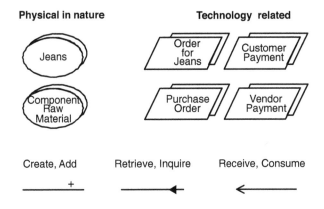

Figure 4.2 Only Denim Jeans Inputs, Outputs, and Connectors

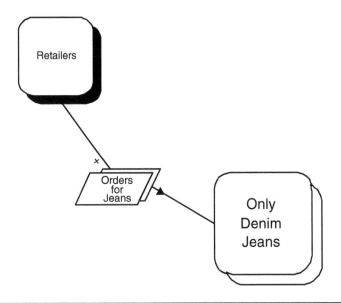

Figure 4.3 Receives Order for Jeans

relationship in Figure 4.3. The create construct is represented by a line with a plus sign (+) on the end of the element being created. The retrieve construct is represented by a line with an arrow on the end near the element being retrieved (Figure 4.3).

The replenishment orders from the retailers are consolidated and purchase orders for component raw materials are created for the numerous vendors and suppliers. We similarly represent this relationship in Figure 4.4.

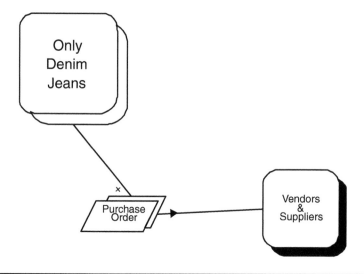

Figure 4.4 Creates Purchase Order

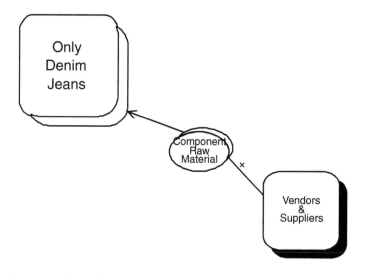

Figure 4.5 Receives Component Raw Material

Sometime later, the vendors and suppliers deliver their component raw materials ordered by The Only Denim Jeans Factory. Receive or consumption is represented by an arrow with the arrowhead on the end toward the element that uses the input. This is most commonly used to represent things such as raw materials used in an activity or process. We represent this relationship in Figure 4.5.

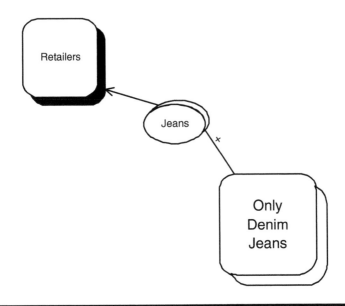

Figure 4.6   Creates Jeans

The Only Denim Jeans Factory then delivers the jeans manufactured to replenish the selling items. We represent this relationship in Figure 4.6.

There are a few other obvious things that we also know, and this is the fun part for The Only Denim Jeans Factory: it gets paid. We represent this relationship in Figure 4.7.

As for the things that are not much fun, The Only Denim Jeans Factory has to pay for its component raw materials. We represent this relationship in Figure 4.8.

It all comes together in Figure 4.9, an architecture model. Even though one can describe and see an instantiation of a workflow, it is still an architecture model and it is static.

We now have the start of a high-level model of The Only Denim Jeans Factory, with a couple of external entities and inputs and outputs indicating core processes included within the enterprise. Further analysis of these core processes identifies two key value streams: *Order-to-Cash* and *Requisition-to-Payables*. Some might prefer the cross-functional process names of *order management* and *procurement*, respectively, but we use the *value stream names* (see Table 5.1, for a complete list).

As we proceed with identification of other inputs and outputs, and decomposition of the enterprise, we will identify other value streams and their relationships with one another and with the external entities. This is the beginning of the enterprise business architecture. We focus on what the enterprise produces, encapsulate the activities into value streams, and

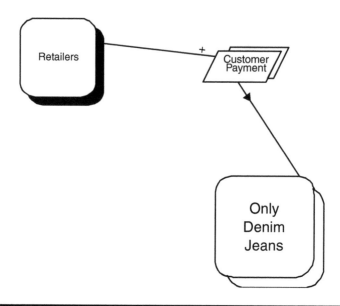

Figure 4.7 Receives Customer Payment

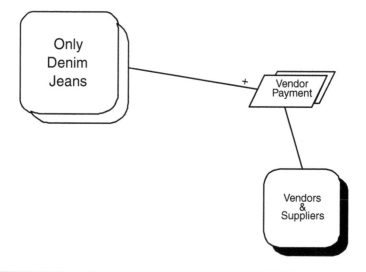

Figure 4.8 Creates Vendor Payment

finally aggregate all of them into the enterprise entity. In addition to this focus, we are building a rich graphical representation of what would normally be a text description. With this approach, we can significantly reduce the amount of textural descriptions and replace them with more

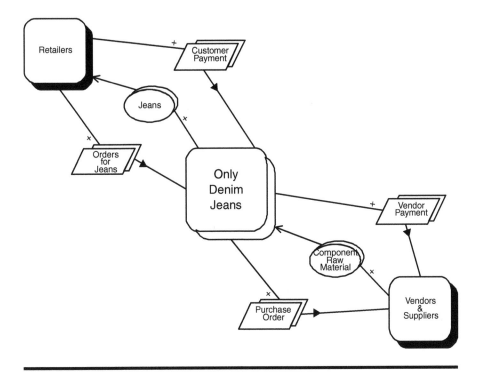

Figure 4.9 Enterprise with Inputs and Outputs

precise models that provide a clearer understanding of the business that is subject to less misinterpretation. A picture is worth a thousand words.

We now have a preliminary model that is slowly developing into something interesting and useful. Again, we must reiterate that the model in Figure 4.9 is an architectural type, *not* a workflow type. Perhaps you can visualize the workflows by looking at the architecture, or perhaps you can describe the workflow to an associate, but this is still an architectural model.

If you were looking at the blueprints of your dream home, you could do the same thing. By looking at the various rooms and layout of your home, you could visualize how to get from one part of the home to the other. You might even decide to move doors or walls or even add windows based on your visualizations and discussions with your spouse and family. For The Only Denim Jeans Factory, we have not illustrated the sequence of activities or the physical means by which some of the inputs are consumed or the outputs produced. It is when we develop the workflow models that the sequence and timing of these activities will become apparent.

The model and textural descriptions imply that a relationship exists between the two value streams, Order-to-Cash and Requisition-to-Payables. The Only Denim Jeans Factory is producing replenishment orders for items that are selling and not building up the retailers' inventory with items that are not selling. The factory is also receiving raw materials to manufacture the replenishment orders in a just-in-time fashion and not building up an inventory of raw materials.

In The Only Denim Jeans Factory EBA, Order-to-Cash and Requisition-to-Payables value streams are integrated by design. Every change in replenishment orders causes a corresponding change in procured raw materials. They begin to co-evolve[4] through each cycle of operation, becoming more inseparable and more dependent on one another until they are one process or system. As they co-evolve, they reach higher levels of effectiveness and efficiency. This behavior occurs within The Only Denim Jeans Factory and quite possibly with the factory's retailers and suppliers as well.

Let us look at using a hypothetical example of The Only Denim Jeans Factory's architecture for an item that is selling really well, striped jeans, and for a product that is not selling well, plaid jeans. Both products were developed by The Only Denim Jeans Factory's R&D team in a value stream called Concept-to-Development.

After careful negotiation with the retailers, The Only Denim Jeans Factory starts production and delivery of striped jeans. They are an instant hit and sales take off. The Only Denim Jeans Factory receives more and more replenishment orders from its retailers and purchases more raw materials to make more striped jeans. By design, the enterprise is built to respond to these increasing demands for any hot selling product. Because production is driven by precise customer demand and not best guesses from the sales people, The Only Denim Jeans Factory optimizes its sales and profit potential.

As for plaid jeans, sales never really take off. Consequently, no replenishment orders are received by The Only Denim Jeans Factory, so it does not order the raw materials for producing more plaid jeans. Here again, by design, the enterprise is built to respond to the lack of demand for any product. In this case, The Only Denim Jeans Factory minimizes its lost sales and lost profit potential, but it does not end here. The factory still has to help its retailers get rid of the initial shipments of plaid jeans through deep discounts and other similar means. Additionally, The Only Denim Jeans Factory has to go back to its R&D team and Concept-to-Development value stream to determine what happened.

Something else of interest is also occurring. Refer to the title of Kevin Kelly's book, *Out of Control*. What does it mean? Usually that phrase is associated with chaos, things gone crazy, and the like. However, you have designed and built control into the process, and consequently, you are out of control. This means that you have designed order and stability into the process. This process is under control by your design and not out of control due to chaotic events. Instead of anticipating demand with your best guesses, you are responding to demand based on accurate sales results. Instead of managing each cycle of operations from the seat of your pants, you are using accurate sales data. This co-evolution (some might prefer *mutualism* or *symbiosis*) requires a dedicated commitment to make it work. If you have finely tuned your business intelligence software, you can speed up the co-evolution process even more.

Every value stream needs the co-evolution capability and a feedback mechanism to analyze performance and make improvements. The enterprise value streams evolve and adapt not just to meet their own needs, but also to meet other value streams' needs and other external entities' needs. This is by design, void of corporate politics and self-serving dysfunctional silos and fiefdoms. Other adjustments, improvements, and tweaks are based in the performance indicators found in the strategy, again designed to optimize sales and profits. The enterprise value streams continue to evolve into a single integrated entity achieving holistic harmony.

So far we have identified only two value streams for The Only Denim Jeans Factory. As we continue to build the entity model with other inputs and outputs, we will start to identify other value streams in the enterprise. Later, we will decompose the enterprise into its various value streams and architectural components. When we finally get to the workflow level, we will design the workflows such that each is formally integrated and connected to one another. This is how we unify the workflows with the architecture.

Hopefully, you have started to understand the capabilities of engineering your enterprise with value streams. To reiterate: A **value stream** is an end-to-end collection of activities that creates a result for a customer, who may be the ultimate customer or an internal end user of the value stream. The value stream has a clear goal: to satisfy or delight the customer.[5] Once the value streams that make up the EBA are defined, we can then start to determine the performance expectations that create alignment with the enterprise strategy. By using a rich modeling language, you can base your performance criteria on the graphically articulated value stream inputs and outputs. For example, you can define metrics and measures for the products produced in the enterprise. You can measure defective units and late orders, for example, all of which are important to the customers of The Only Denim Jeans Factory. These can then tie back to the strategic objectives of customer satisfaction, customer retention, and increased market share.

As you probably can surmise, The Only Denim Jeans Factory's vision is to become the worldwide leader in its market. The objectives of improving customer service, increasing market share, and bringing new products to market all support this vision. We can easily establish performance criteria for each value stream as it applies or influences the objectives.

The value streams enable the alignment of the results delivered by the enterprise in support of the corporate strategy and vision. This is a formidable task to undertake using only the organization chart or a business function/process model (refer to Figure 2.3). In addition, it is extremely hard to co-evolve functions with one another with no clear understanding of the ultimate goals and objectives of the enterprise.

A NEW BEHAVIOR

To create a competitive advantage, we need to envision new customer-centric products and services. We need to think differently, to break out of the old ways of doing things. We need to think about what is important to the customer, all the while maintaining alignment and focus with the whole enterprise. As noted in Chapter 3, we have many tough questions to answer, for example:

- How do customers view our enterprise?
- How do the stakeholders view our enterprise?
- How does our enterprise achieve the corporate objectives?
- How do we enable and support our enterprise?
- How do our employees view our enterprise?
- How do we increase profit?
- How do we increase market share?
- How do we develop new products and services?
- How do we improve productivity?
- How do we reduce costs?

None of the answers to these questions are found in a single functional organization or department within the enterprise. To find the answers, one must cobble together a solution in an ad hoc fashion from several functional organizations and departments. Today's enterprises, for the most part, are not integrated, aligned, or able to effectively or efficiently answer these questions.

We have to find ways to integrate all aspects of the enterprise together, holistically, supported by sound strategic planning. Otherwise, we are just chasing a moving target. We sometimes get distracted with a new corporate reorganization or a fiscal fitness initiative. Perhaps some "hot" Web project is causing the distraction. Regardless, we must maintain our focus on the customer and keep the enterprise aligned.

We need a new approach and a new solution that is viewed and judged from the customer perspective. We need one that is comprehensive and inclusive of people, processes, and technologies, integrated from strategy to results. We also need a new and improved architecture — the enterprise business architecture — one that focuses on the customer, creates unity of purpose, manifests the vision, is holistic in nature, is integrated, and is the mother of all architectures.

We need to understand the enterprise holistically and keep it aligned in all of its complex dimensions. We need people who can think in multiple dimensions. Some people in the enterprise can only understand their functional chain of command, vertically up and down the organization chart. These thinkers are called "liners" and are able to see in only one dimension. Others have a better view of the enterprise, a cross-functional view, understanding what goes on in their department and other departments as well. These thinkers are called "flatlanders," existing in a pre-1492 world that is flat, waiting for Columbus to prove that the Earth is round. But this is the 21st century.

A few others can think in another, or third, dimension about the customers and suppliers. They can see the impact of enterprise actions on customer satisfaction, customer service, and supplier relations. And finally, a very few can articulate the enterprise in its fourth dimension: time. Time to market, getting new products and services to market, is critical to growth and survival. You have to beat the competition in all four dimensions every day. You have to harness the power of the enterprise and build a value-creating system out of the value streams. This is a difficult, if not impossible, task to achieve strictly from the organizational chart or the business function/process model.

You have to understand and measure the contributions of all value streams in all four dimensions. The co-evolution of the value streams described earlier must take all four dimensions into account. If we cause something to change in a value stream, we must be able to predict the effects in other values streams. We cannot make the change and then wait a month to see what happens. Leading and running an enterprise is not a spectator sport.

We have all heard some of the silly stories about the single-minded functional thinkers or liners. For example, after reading a book on just-in-time management, the raw materials manager decided to slow down the procurement and stockpiling of raw materials until the production line was finally screaming for parts. This manager just did not think about the impact of this decision on customers, as well as other departments within the enterprise. After all, this action was simply going to reduce the costs associated with maintaining raw materials.

From a fiscal fitness point of view, the manager probably was rewarded for this action. This manager, however, failed to foresee the impact on production, late deliveries to customers, and the other delays associated with getting a new product out of R&D. Obviously, this liner mentality unchecked can create serious problems for the enterprise.

Expand the existing views of the enterprise to include all four business dimensions: from within departments and organizations that are efficient and adaptive; from across the enterprise, including all departments and organizations that collectively deliver value; from the point of view of our customers and suppliers; and from time to market and beating the competition. View the enterprise in terms of results, not just activities, with a customer-centric perspective. Decompose the enterprise and then reaggregate it using value streams, measure each value stream in all four dimensions where appropriate, link these measures with the strategic objectives of the enterprise, and integrate people, process, and technology throughout the enterprise.

Seeing the enterprise in all four dimensions is possible with a business architecture based on value stream thinking. Within the models, you have all the relationships described just as in the blueprint of your dream home. A customer-centric view combined with the appropriate metrics and measures helps to determine which courses of action to take and predict the outcomes of decisions in terms of contributions to all four dimensions of the enterprise.

The use of a rich graphical notation enables precise communications and descriptions of architectures, workflows, and events. You build a holistic enterprise model that all enterprise employees can understand, analyze, and use to build a competitive advantage. Everyone begins to think in all four dimensions, understanding the causes and effects of their decisions. This, coupled with a keen understanding of the corporate strategy, keeps every initiative aligned and focused. Now the EBA is alive.

When more research and analysis is required, you have the ability to explore the current framework of models and their decomposed lower levels to seek out additional insight, improvements, and efficiencies. The understanding gained from this analysis helps determine the changes to people, processes, and technologies throughout the enterprise. We then renew or update all of the accepted and integrated models and release the new version as the basis for the next round of enhancements. Then we do it all over again.

This is not a one-time event, but rather an ongoing process. Corporate leadership must evolve the enterprise over and over again, initially responding to market forces and later influencing market forces. This evolution requires the enterprise to develop into a learning organization, as described by Peter Senge in *The Fifth Discipline*.[6] At the heart of the learning organization is a shift of mind — from seeing ourselves as separate from the world to connected to the world, from seeing problems as caused by someone or something "out there" to seeing how our actions create the problems we experience.

The fifth discipline is systems thinking. It is a framework for seeing patterns of change rather than static snapshots, and for seeing interrelationships rather than things. It is a discipline for seeing the structures that underlie complex situations, a way to discern high-leverage from low-leverage change, and, finally, a discipline for seeing wholes not just parts.[7] Systems thinking and viewing the enterprise in all four dimensions is not a project phase, but a new corporate behavior. A behavior requires sage leadership and constant nurturing. If implemented and sustained properly, it quite possibly may develop into one of the enterprise's differentiators or core competencies in the marketplace.

WHAT NEW CAPABILITIES ARE POSSIBLE WITH THE EBA?

The EBA has a well-thought-out composition, a boundary, and a definition, but it is not intended to confine, limit, or restrict strategy, but rather to open it up, to free it from existing paradigms, and to enable one to imagine possibilities from a holistic perspective. These new capabilities come from the use of the EBA as a tool for building and creating a value-creating system, rather than from the tool itself.

The obvious advantage of the EBA is its logical structure, but its primary usefulness is found in its ability to focus and stimulate the imagination. Out of the boundaries of the architecture we find enhanced and new capabilities from current and new relationships that were once misunderstood, inconceivable, or unthinkable. Once the relationships and requirements are understood or envisioned, we are able to define these enhanced or new capabilities. Success is then measured based on improvements in customer service, stakeholder value, and profit. So the true value of the architecture is found not in the model itself, but in its ability to communicate a shared understanding about the future, its ability to unify the enterprise with its engineered design and holistic strategy.

The strategy, coupled with the EBA, provides an advantage over the competition. You can create more effective and efficient results with the tool than your competitors because they probably do not have an EBA. Of course, it depends on how you use this tool to create that advantage. Posting it in the cafeteria and executive offices accomplishes little. Disseminating it throughout the enterprise, changing corporate behavior, and thinking holistically will deliver the desired results. It is using the tool each day that delivers these results. Look at the EBA in terms of possibilities and new ways of servicing your customers, limited only by your imagination.

In an EBA workshop a few years ago, a participant approached us from the Business Continuity Project team. Although we knew of her background, we were unfamiliar with her project work. She made quite a surprising statement. She said that if she had had the EBA before her business continuity engagement began, that she could have reduced the engagement time and cost by three to six weeks for a business unit. During the first few weeks of her engagement, she had to develop an equivalent EBA of sorts to base her business continuity recommendations on core processes that must sustain the business in spite of a catastrophe. She had to have a holistic focus on the enterprise, not a "pieces and parts" view. For example, protecting some of the more critical functional financial processes is not enough. One also has to protect all of the other activities and processes that deal with order fulfillment so one can stay in business.

Here is an example of a new capability surfacing out of the EBA, one that we had never considered. It came from a holistic thinker, a four-dimensional thinker viewing the architecture not as just a model, but as a tool for understanding the critical nature of business continuity, disaster recovery, and business regeneration.

The example we used previously described a fictitious enterprise, The Only Denim Jeans Factory. However, we can use the same approach to describe a real extended enterprise architecture with it customers and suppliers or any external entity that requires process improvement. The same modeling concepts, approaches, and language constructs can build just about any extended enterprise, virtual enterprise, business web, or value net. Usually the EBA is used for analysis of a particular enterprise, as was described in the example.

As another example, we can use the EBA to model and understand the architectural relationships between a credit card holder, a merchant, and the various banks that process a credit card transaction. In this example, we are more interested in the relationships between the external entities than those internal to the enterprise. In a PBS show called *Electric Money*,[8] the story describes most of the activities and relationships that take place when someone uses his bank's credit card to make a purchase from a merchant who accepts that particular credit card's business. Refer to Figure 4.10.

Perhaps in this analysis, we are particularly interested in the response time it takes to process the transaction among all of the external entities. After all, effective and efficient business processes are critical between external enterprises as well as within our enterprise. Our focus in this example is building a network capable of supporting subsecond response time among several external enterprises. Here we have an extended

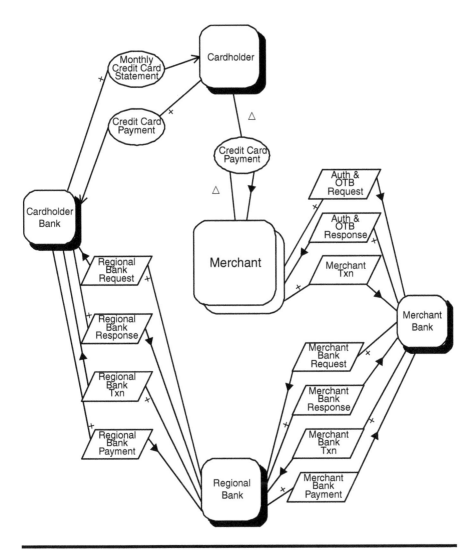

Figure 4.10 Merchant Credit Card Model

enterprise architecture relative to the merchant, illustrating the relationships between:

- The cardholder and the merchant
- The merchant and the merchant's bank
- The merchant's bank and the credit card's regional bank
- The credit card's regional bank and the cardholder's bank
- The cardholder's bank and the cardholder

It is possible to understand and extrapolate some of the workflow activities from this architecture model. Again, just as we can visualize how to go from room to room from the blueprints of our dream home, we can visualize the transaction flow of messages from external entity to external entity across the network. The architecture model makes the understanding of the business comprehensible, and it may even encourage the analysis of some of the internal workflow models to find more opportunities for improving performance across the entire network. Consider this: Is it possible to glean the same understanding and perform the same process analysis from a textural description of this process? Can you conduct the analysis more accurately and with less misinterpretation using only text?

Can you envision new capabilities, products, and service offerings from the enterprise business architecture? Can you envision performance improvements and a competitive advantage in your marketplace? Can you imagine a "room with a view of the future" from your dream home? Are you ready for some new and creative ideas and perhaps a few pleasant surprises along the way?

REFERENCES

1. Rudy Rucker, *The Fourth Dimension: A Guided Tour of the Higher Universes* (Boston: Houghton Mifflin, 1984), 18.
2. Joel Arthur Barker, *Discovering the Future: The Business of Paradigms* (St. Paul, MN: I.L.I. Press, 1989), 12–15.
3. Kevin Kelly, *Out of Control: The Rise of Neo-Biological Civilization* (Reading, MA: Addison-Wesley, 1994), 188.
4. Ibid., 73–77.
5. James Martin, *The Great Transition: Using the Seven Disciplines of Enterprise Engineering to Align People, Technology, and Strategy* (New York: American Management Association, 1995), 104.
6. Peter M. Senge, *The Fifth Discipline: The Art and Practice of the Learning Organization* (New York: Doubleday, 1990), 12–13.
7. Ibid., 68–69.
8. *Electric Money*, Oregon Public Broadcasting, 2001.

II

CASE STUDY

5

BUILDING THE ENTERPRISE BUSINESS ARCHITECTURE

SELECTING A CASE STUDY EXAMPLE

For the case study, consider another fictitious company, *Widget, Inc.*, a mid-cap-size enterprise, similar to The Only Denim Jeans Factory, selling its products to customers worldwide. The case study is simplified quite a bit to explain the concepts of an enterprise business architecture (EBA) without getting lost in complex details. However, it does contain enough detail to demonstrate proof of concept and to illustrate some real-world complexity. We could have modeled a lemonade stand and very easily demonstrated the concepts; however, it is doubtful that the lemonade stand would stand up to any serious examination or provide enough variety for analysis.

The Widget, Inc., case study model is *not* a recommendation for a typical order-to-build manufacturing enterprise, but a teaching aid. It more closely represents an "as is" model rather than a "to be" model, but it is fairly up to date in terms of current technology. Over the years we have incorporated some of our experiences from real engagements into the models to help with the teaching aspects. We settled on a typical manufacturing example because it was an early experience with a large enterprise and one that contained numerous references from other books and literature. The base models were used on every EBA engagement as a starting point, a source of reference, and intellectual capital.

The models in this book were developed in Visio® using a specifically designed Enterprise Business Architecture — Modeling Language (EBA-ML) stencil and template. We decided to use Visio because it is a fairly popular and available software product and priced economically for the typical user. Visio easily ports the models to a standard Web format for viewing by all enterprise personnel on the intranet. Some have criticized this decision for selecting a simple graphical product like Visio; however, the purchase of an expensive industrial-strength modeling tool is beyond the justification and reach of many small and midsize companies. Besides, the current selection of modeling tools merely captures your thoughts and ideas, and does not do any thinking for you. The modeling tools topic will get some attention later.

This case study is *not* a user type manual or a detailed how-to set of instructions, but an overview of the EBA of a typical enterprise. It is assumed by the authors that the reader has a fairly good understanding of workflow modeling and its basic principles. The case study's purpose is to provide an example set of EBA models for review and analysis, but not for use as a set of mechanical steps for building one.

USING THE INTELLECTUAL CAPITAL

Although the primary purpose of the case study is to illustrate the approach and rules for developing an EBA, you may also use it as an early draft of your particular EBA. Developing an EBA from scratch without any intellectual capital is a timely and costly undertaking, so consider using this case study as a start. It can save you some time and money, while giving you a textbook example to follow.

Because the EBA is the formal or missing link between the business models and information technology (IT) models, getting started trying to define something that is missing is quite difficult. Modeling the whole enterprise or business unit is no small undertaking either. James Martin's book *The Great Transition*[1] serves as an excellent starting point for defining, building, and integrating the value streams. In his book he lists 17 value streams for a typical manufacturing enterprise. This is where we began in developing our intellectual capital. Over the past few years, we have updated, enhanced, deleted, and completely rebuilt the intellectual capital, but the value streams have held true and are always the foundation and starting point.

Table 5.1 summarizes the candidate value streams for Widget, Inc., that we chose from our intellectual capital. All value stream names use the same format in the title, such as *Order-to-Cash* and *Prospect-to-Customer*. Numerous books and texts use this kind of core process title, for example, *Reengineering the Corporation*, by Michael Hammer and James Champy.[2]

The first part of the value stream name represents the beginning or initial point of the process and the last part represents the ending or final point. Just do not spend too much time naming the baby, as you are trying to use a short, catchy phrase to represent a rather large collection

Table 5.1   Value Streams and Cross-Functional Names

Value Streams	Typical Cross-Functional Names
Prospect-to-Customer	Customer engagement
Order-to-Cash	Order fulfillment
Manufacturing-to-Distribution	Operations and logistics
Request-to-Service	Customer service
Insight-to-Strategy	Strategic planning
Vision-to-eBusiness Enterprise	Enterprise management
Concept-to-Development	R&D, product and service evolution
Initiative-to-Results	Implementation execution
Relationship-to-Partnership	Strategic partnering and outsourcing
Forecast-to-Plan	Budgeting, outlooks and forecasting
Requisition-to-Payables	Procurement/vendor management
Resource availability-to-Consumption	Resource management
Acquisition-to-Obsolescence	Fixed-asset management
Financial close-to-Reporting	Finance and accounting
Recruitment-to-Retirement	Human resource management
Awareness-to-Prevention	Quality and safety management

of processes and activities. A new term, such as *value streams*, and a new title, such as *Order-to-Cash*, help us to break away from the domain of functional thinking. Additionally, we provided the typical cross-functional process names associated with the value stream names for orientation purposes only. The terms are generally used by people already thinking in value stream terms, but unaware of James Martin's formal definition. Refer to Table 5.1 as a transitional document and quickly try to get people to use the "Order-to-Cash" type names.

Although we always think that our business unit, enterprise, and industry are unique, there are numerous similarities from the value stream prospective. Widget, Inc., which is a manufacturing model, was once used to start an engagement with a software development company. On another occasion, we used Widget, Inc., on a healthcare engagement. Another team used Widget, Inc., on a telecom engagement. In all of these engagements, Widget, Inc., served as a realistic case study for training and later as an early EBA draft for the real engagement with only a modicum of changes.

It seems that when a client team can start with a reasonably complete and consistent model, the evolution to their specific model progresses much more quickly. The most difficult and time-consuming experience we had was trying to build the EBA up from the functional models of order entry, credit authorization, and scheduling. Trying to build the *whole* from a loose association of *parts* was extremely difficult, but starting from a top-down approach, we found that you can minimize this difficulty, maintain focus on the enterprise, and reinforce the behavior of holistic thinking.

In actuality, after you get the value streams fairly well defined, you can shift the emphasis to them without losing the perspective of the whole enterprise. You may even choose to select a few key value streams to start the EBA, for example, those that are customer facing, and later select the others in a priority sequence based on the needs of the enterprise.

Some clients prefer to start at a business unit level rather than the enterprise level. This is certainly acceptable, and in large corporations desirable, as long as you keep the business units in context of the whole enterprise and maintain a holistic view. You may even use the first business unit's models to start the second business unit, and so on. Then your next question is, How do I combine the multiple business unit models into only one enterprise model?

Combining the models is not the most important issue. Getting all business units to optimize performance in accordance with the strategic objectives is the most important issue. If you can combine the models, then fine. Otherwise, focus on meeting and exceeding the performance measures and building a value-creating system. A sustained competitive advantage from separate models is far more important than a combined model with fewer results. Use the EBA as a tool to achieve that competitive advantage and measure the positive impact on the strategic objectives as an indication of success.

You may already have some existing models, diagrams, and representations of the enterprise. Collect and analyze them, as some may prove informative and valuable in building the EBA. If you have a variety of workflow models, you may have to reclassify them within a value stream. This does not mean that you have to redraw them all, but you may want to modify some to integrate them into the EBA. Connections are based on inputs and outputs. So if you have a lower-level model in another format with the inputs and outputs well defined, then integration into the EBA is achievable without redrawing.

Remember, this approach recognizes that the embedded base of models, diagrams, and documentation is useful and seeks to integrate the parts into the whole without having to redraw everything. Different IT domains use different disciplines. Your legacy domain, computer-aided software engineering (CASE) domain, object-oriented domain, and Web domain are all different and represent a sizable investment of resources. Seek out ways to integrate these different domains from a higher level without having to toss what you already have.

BUILDING AN EBA TEAM

The most important contribution that senior executives can make to the development of the EBA is their personal commitment. The manifestation of this commitment is demonstrated by finding team members with the right skills and dedicating talented people to the effort, setting reasonable expectations with regard to resources and schedules, and actually supporting the development and use of the architectures in strategic planning sessions. With this kind of leadership, the architectures will not only get through the initial development phases, but also evolve into the norm for conducting business at the strategic, tactical, and operational levels of the enterprise.

A key ingredient in building integrated enterprise architectures is a committed, well-rounded, and collaborative team:

- The senior executives must assign a full-time *EBA leader*. An outside consultant may initially fill this role, but an in-house leader needs to later assume the EBA responsibility, as it will require ongoing, long-term support and maintenance once the initial release is built.
- You also need to assign a *full-time lead facilitator and modeler* to direct the architecture development effort. These two individuals must plan to rotate responsibilities, and each must acquire the other's proficiency. This provides balance and prevents fatigue.
- A background in business analysis and/or software development provides a *team member* with an important foundation for supporting the integrated enterprise architectures. Pairing up a "business type" with an "IT type" builds a very synergistic and collaborative team. In a best-case scenario, they are subject matter experts who are very knowledgeable about the enterprise and the operations of the company. They should also have contacts in organizations throughout the company and know other subject matter experts. Building an enterprise team is critical to completing the EBA and making it an operational reality.

The roles and responsibilities of the team members are detailed as follows:

- *EBA leader*: This individual needs a broad background and experience in several operational areas of the enterprise. More importantly, this person needs to report to a high-level executive and have all of the necessary authority, responsibility, and accountability to develop and maintain the EBA. The typical characteristics of a good leader are necessary and important for this position.

One other leadership characteristic that is essential to developing a successful EBA is the ability to work with people from all over the enterprise, from all levels within the organizations, and possibly across international borders. The leader must prove to be credible and possess and instill holistic and systems thinking behaviors in all participants and organizations. He or she must bring divergent organizations and regions together to form an enterprise team focused on enterprise goals. The leader must be persistent and undaunted by adversity because getting functional representatives to think about the overall enterprise first is a difficult and often painful undertaking.

■ *Lead facilitator.* This individual must have knowledge of and experience in enterprise modeling. However, any kind of formal modeling and facilitating experiences are a big plus. The skilled facilitator, preferably a modeler, must keep the sessions moving, making measurable progress, collecting information, and providing a little entertainment along the way. He or she must make sessions interesting and challenging for the participants, and make ample use of past experiences and illustrative stories or case studies from supporting reference materials and books.

Look for ways to increase collaboration among the participants and between different teams developing other value streams. Once some level of detail is captured, enforce the behavior of constantly balancing and leveling the models both horizontally, connecting each model with other value streams and external entities, and vertically, updating each level of the model with the external inputs and outputs.

■ *Modeler* (using Visio or similar graphics tool): This individual has the thankless task of capturing the hand-written scribbles off the white board and turning the raw data into an easily understood model. Always strive to present the models in their best cosmetic form. The appearance of the models is a compromise of several conflicting preferences. Try to keep outputs close to their inputs, minimize crossed lines, avoid bunching up several shapes or connectors in one part of the model, and spread the model out over a larger worksheet when the model gets crowded.

EBA development requires expertise in the following skills:

■ *Listening*: This is the most important and necessary skill. It requires the facilitator to hear and understand the participants' comments and suggestions. It is sometimes difficult to listen, interpret the participants' comments, and diagram their thoughts on the models all at the same time. It is OK to ask the participants to slow down or to repeat things they say so that you can catch up in the modeling. Just ensure that their comments are heard, collected as data, and somehow captured on the model. You may decide later to "scrub the data" and modify it in the context of other information, but just ensure that you capture their thoughts. Use note boxes as appropriate and even log action items with the responsible individual on the models themselves.

■ *Facilitating*: This skill requires you to keep the participants interested in the models and actively providing information. Each participant needs to feel free to express any idea or provide any data, even though it is inflammatory or negative. After all, this is how you get to the root causes of problems and discover new opportunities. In some cases, the facilitator is a manager or former manager of a participant. Ensure that the facilitator checks his or her title at the door. Worry less about the room arrangement and seating and more on how the people are responding. New facilitators may consider a book or class on facilitation or body language. Experience in conducting joint application development (JAD) sessions is a big plus and a very desirable trait.

■ *Modeling*: The constructs of a disciplined modeling language require a thorough understanding of each shape's or line's syntax and semantics. This enables the facilitator to efficiently transform textural descriptions into graphical models. However, occasions will occur that will prevent you from capturing the participants' comments. Just describe their thoughts in a temporary note box and keep moving. You can update the model later after you have had a chance to discuss it or review it outside of the meeting. You may choose to introduce the modeling language slowly, using the more frequently used constructs and introducing the others as you progress. If the modeling language is well structured and well defined, it is usually picked up very quickly through on-the-job type exposure. However, attendance in a short concepts and training class usually gets all participants in the modeling activities up to speed quickly. Taking the class significantly improves the teams' ability to grasp modeling concepts and the techniques, and allows them to more readily focus on the content of the models rather than technique.

The above describes the key players in EBA development. However, also needed are several participants to serve on value stream teams. The team composition consists of the following profiles:

■ *Participants*: The background of the participants is similar to the ones described above. Those who have experience in operational areas or as business analysts or software developers are excellent candidates. Here again, pair up a "business type" with an "IT type" in the teams. These pairs really work well together and stimulate one another's thinking. We sometimes refer to this pair as the paradigm twins. They are directed by the EBA leader, the paradigm shifter.[3] In some cases, you just need to turn them loose on the enterprise, looking for performance improvements and ways to gain a competitive advantage. They have a marvelous opportunity to contribute not only to their value stream, but also to the whole enterprise.

EBA sessions require extensive and careful preparation so that you can get active and enthusiastic participation by the various team members and achieve anticipated results. The following preworkshop activities are critical to a productive and meaningful session:

■ *Review the intellectual capital*: This is the most important preparation you can make. This base of information provides you with insight, patterns, and thought-provoking questions to ask the participants. It will speed up your modeling efforts and offer the most efficient approach to synthesizing the information captured in modeling sessions. Even if you are comparing the intellectual capital from a service industry with your current product-oriented industry, you can get started faster and keep moving much better than if you were beginning the modeling effort with a blank white board.

■ *Analyze the current models*: This requires the facilitator to spend some quality time reviewing the models, their connections to other value stream models, and their hierarchical relationships within the value streams. The facilitator must stay ahead of the participants. Sometimes when you get several teams modeling concurrently this can be a challenge because once they get the hang of it, their output can become enormous. When the JAD type session starts, set expectations at the beginning, and at the end, plan the next session. Assign action items or homework when appropriate.

■ *Prepare for getting bogged down*: Depending on several factors such as a shy participant, a threatened participant, or group reticence, you may find yourself unable to make progress. You may find yourself stuck and unable to get any active participation out of the team. When this occurs, shift away from the model toward the lexicons and take the team back to the "What do you produce?" type discussions. This is the best action to take when the team seems to slow down or even stop discussing the scheduled topic.

You may even try to get individual participants to take ownership of one or two lexicons for development outside the meeting. Try to assign a lexicon to a participant who produces or uses it in his daily work. Subtly send a message that if you do not get participation, then they will get homework. If this does not work, then move up, down, or to the side of the model (or level), or even go to their workflow model. Find a more interesting or even entertaining model to develop. Consider letting the team pick the model to develop. You will eventually need all the information anyway, so this approach does not seriously affect the overall progress of the modeling.

Remember, you have to adapt to the participants' willingness and ability to provide information. Ensure that you have provided a safe, nonthreatening environment for problem identification and a creative atmosphere for improvement ideas.

When is the EBA really implemented? It is implemented when all major strategic initiatives are analyzed and prioritized through analysis of the architectures. You start to see the architectures both "as is" and "to be" in the initiative document. Because the impact of the initiative is evaluated on its contributions to the whole enterprise, the political posturing between organizations begins to subside. The reason to undertake the initiative is based on its expectations and desired results, not the latest new whiz-bang technology or personal preference of an executive. Instead of having the executives competing with one another for funding and priority, you have them challenging the competition for market share and profit.

THE PROCESS STEPS AND MODEL LEVELS

This section will provide you with a brief overview of how to build the EBA. These steps are based on actual experience gained during several engagements and working with different industries. This basic approach is adaptive to just about any enterprise. Although the approach may appear strictly top-down in nature, this is not an absolute. Typically, we will start from the top of the EBA, but as we get further into the modeling effort, you will see that the approach is very iterative and not only top-down, but bottom-up and middle-out.

Once you get the foundation and first draft of the value streams, you may expand the model based on corporate priorities and needs. Value streams will evolve at different speeds; some will mature quickly and some will simply serve as placeholders until your priorities allow their development. Your analysis of enterprise strategic initiatives will provide keen insight into the setting of priorities for value stream analysis.

Refer to Table 5.2 for a quick overview of the steps in EBA development. In this example, assume that we will develop a handful of selected

Table 5.2   EBA Steps and Levels

EBA Steps	Level of Model	Comments
1. Building the enterprise entity	1	One entity per enterprise
2. Recognizing the value streams	4	Estimate 16–24, a peer level model
3. Aggregating the value streams	2 and 3	Minimum of two levels Level 2 — one per enterprise Level 3 — one per group aggregate (usually 3–6 groups)
4. Determining the business use cases	4	Estimate 4–10, per value stream, a peer level model
5. Identifying the business events	4	Estimate 16–24, one for each value stream, a peer level model
6. Modeling the workflows	5+	Multiple levels depending on scope and complexity

value streams, not all of the enterprise value streams. The level of model (the position in the level of decomposition or aggregation moving from the enterprise entity down to the workflows) is noted as information in the table. As you can see, there is some skipping between levels, so just remember the iterative nature of the EBA development process. You may also refer to Appendix B to see a typical EBA project schedule.

WHAT ARE YOU BUILDING?

Before we rush into the *how* you build an EBA, perhaps we need a brief review of *what* we are going to build. Refer to Figure 5.1. This represents the various models and their hierarchical relationships to one another. This is the bill of processes referred to earlier. This will only represent part of the model, a vertical section, to keep it understandable in the context of this case study. However, in a real engagement, you will completely fill out the hierarchy with all of the models, as previously represented in Figure 3.5. Clients sometimes refer to this hierarchy model as the "mall map" and place a "you are here" sticker on the appropriate modeling level during presentations. This same model also provides the schema for Visio and Web navigation.

The first four levels of the EBA are architecture levels. Level 4, the peer level of models, begins a transition from the architecture to the workflow. At level 4, you have an event model, the last level of the value

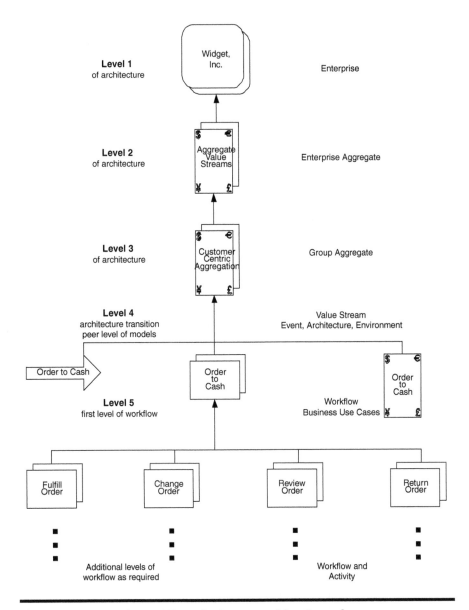

Figure 5.1   Enterprise — Hierarchy Decomposition Example

stream architecture, and the environment model. The workflows of the business use cases (the decomposition of the value stream architectures) start at level 5. At this level you may continue development down until you get to the individual tasks and activities, or you may transition to another IT domain, such as the Unified Modeling Language (UML)/Rational

Unified Process (RUP), a packaged software, a CASE environment, or a legacy environment.

BUILDING THE ENTERPRISE ENTITY

Let us start with a few assumptions about what intellectual capital, models, and diagrams you already have on hand. Refer to Table 5.1. We may initially assume that this material gives you a very general idea or early draft of what is inside the Widget, Inc., entity. These candidate value streams will start to take shape as you connect them to their respective external entities and other internal value streams.

Next, we need a list of all of the external entities that exchange inputs and outputs with the enterprise. This represents the external environment of Widget, Inc. Here you may start to classify or group the external entities according to some similarities. For example, you can group all state, local, and federal organizations into a single external entity called *governmental agencies*. In a similar fashion, you can group all product and service providers into *vendors and suppliers*. Just start listing and classifying the external entities. When you get to the lower levels of the models, you may find it more appropriate to decompose an external entity to illustrate a specific point or to analyze an opportunity.

Once you have a good list of classified or grouped external entities, place them around the Widget, Inc., entity as illustrated in Figure 5.2. It is strongly recommended that the customer be placed at the top, as this maintains the customer-centric focus. You may place the other external entities based on personal preference. However, as the models mature and expand, you may find it necessary to relocate the various external entities to complement the cosmetic nature of the model. Please remember one critical point: *getting the information properly included in the model takes precedence over cosmetics*. Never compromise the accuracy of the information modeled for cosmetic purposes.

For each external entity, start expanding the model with the various inputs and outputs exchanged between the external entities and the enterprise. Use the appropriate connecting EBA-ML constructs such as **creates** and **retrieves** to illustrate the relationships between the inputs, outputs, external entities, and the enterprise. This kind of information usually surfaces quickly in a facilitated JAD type session with knowledgeable participants. Hopefully, you will identify numerous inputs and outputs from the JAD type session. The entity begins to take shape, getting richer in detail and information provided. Refer to Figure 5.3, which illustrates this point.

In building the EBA, we start with the enterprise entity, but will not follow an exact top-down development approach. The approach is far

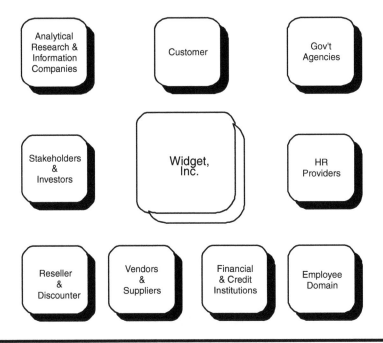

Figure 5.2 Case Study Enterprise and External Entities

more iterative in nature than a one-time top-down pass. As you discover the inputs and outputs, you will find yourself simultaneously thinking about which value stream(s) create and use them.

For example, you see that the customer creates a *customer order request* and that the enterprise receives the request. Because the **aggregated technology input/output** construct is used to represent the *customer order request*, you know that this is a technology type input representing several different but similar kinds of requests. However, at this high level you do not know if the order is placed over the Web or phone, but just that it uses some kind of technology. At this point, you do not have to be more specific because you are after logical structure, not physical detail. You also see that a *fulfilled order* output is created by the enterprise and is received by the customer. Here, because the *fulfilled order* is a real, tangible thing, we use the **aggregated physical input/output** construct to represent the several different types of orders that are fulfilled by the enterprise for the customer.

Look at the *purchase order* created by the enterprise. This is another example of a technology type output created for the *vendors and suppliers*. Also, refer to the *component raw material* and note that it is represented as a real, physical thing created by the *vendors and suppliers*. With regard to the enterprise, you see that it is received and changed. The enterprise

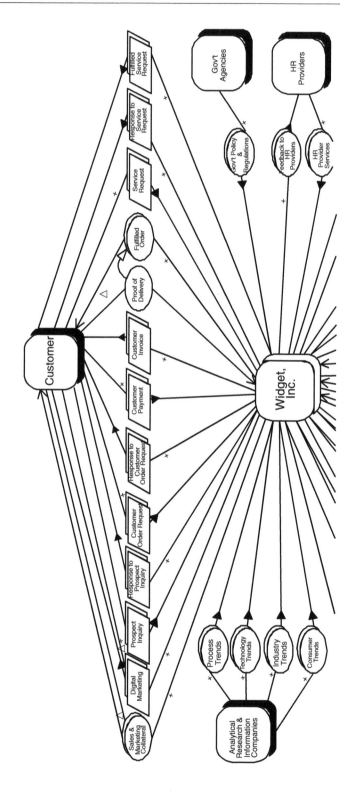

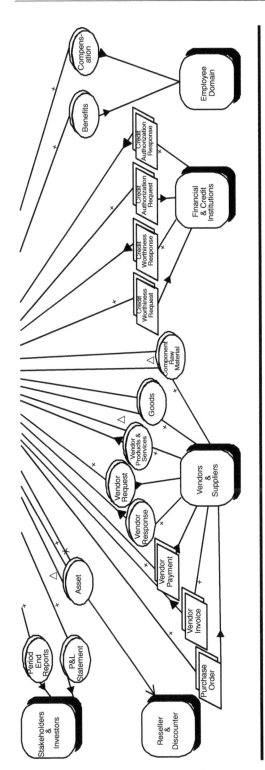

Figure 5.3 Case Study Enterprise with Inputs and Outputs

receives the physical item and changes its location from the receiving dock to the appropriate receiving area.

In your workshop session, continue asking the following questions:

- What does the enterprise produce?
- What does the enterprise consume?
- What are the sources and destinations of the inputs and outputs?

Move around the entity to each external entity and continue thinking about the enterprise value streams, which by their very nature give clues as to what inputs and outputs might be required to satisfy the external entities. Eventually, you exhaust the knowledge of the workshop participants and have to continue in another direction. At this point, you have an early draft of the entity with its inputs and outputs connected with the enterprise's external entities. You are off to an excellent start. You will apply this same technique for all processes and activities, trying to get the participants thinking about *what each produces.*

You may want to occasionally improve the model's appearance once a certain amount of detail is added. This is fine, but do not spend too much time here until the model gets reasonably complete and stable.

The entity is the highest-level model for the enterprise or business unit under analysis. As the model matures, you will find the numbers of inputs and outputs growing significantly. Periodically, review the inputs and outputs for ways to aggregate them into higher levels of information. As described earlier, the aggregation and decomposition of both data and process are the keys to building the comprehensible higher and lower levels of models.

The higher you are in the hierarchy, the more aggregation you will have to do. However, never aggregate simply to reduce the number of inputs and outputs in the model. For example, the *fulfilled order* will consist of the ordered item, its instruction manual, its warranty, its shipping container, and its shipping documents. These logically fit together and are nicely aggregated into the *fulfilled order.* Aggregating *fulfilled order* with *sales and marketing collateral* may reduce the numbers of inputs and outputs, but these two do not logically fit together. They really do not share any aggregation relationships, and each is produced by a different value stream.

Whenever you aggregate or decompose an input or output, you must document the information. You use the lexicon models for this purpose. Refer to Figure 5.4. In this model you describe in detail all of the information about the *fulfilled order.* The lexicon itself may consist of several elements of information and detail. This reduces the necessity to use the *fulfilled order* with all of its detail in a higher-level model and

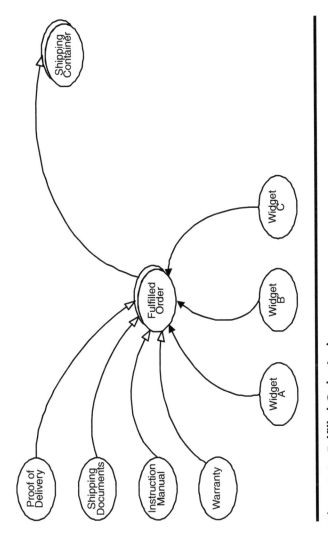

Figure 5.4   Fulfilled Order Lexicon

keeps the models simpler and easier to understand. The person reviewing the model may then choose to look at lower levels of detail when appropriate.

With an early draft of the Widget, Inc., entity, you are ready to start thinking about the individual value streams. You will actually skip a couple of levels in the hierarchy because you need the understanding of the value streams for your particular enterprise before you build the second and third levels (the aggregate value streams and customer centric aggregate value streams, respectively).

RECOGNIZING THE VALUE STREAMS

Assuming you have used this book's intellectual capital or at least referenced James Martin's book, you have a list of candidate value streams. Perhaps this is a good time for you to reread Chapter 7 in *The Great Transition.*[4] This review will help you think about the value streams as you analyze and connect the inputs and outputs. Just refer to Table 5.1 for some of the more familiar cross-functional names that map to value streams. This review may help stimulate your thinking and help the transition to value stream concepts.

It is also a good time to build the first draft of the enterprise hierarchy model based on your intellectual capital. The model in Figure 5.5 describes the decomposition of your enterprise with all of its value streams. This is also an early draft and may change as your EBA matures. At least it gives you a big-picture snapshot of how your enterprise is starting to evolve.

You are now ready to begin building the value stream environment models. We will come back to the two levels between the entity and value streams later, once we understand the enterprise a little better.

Begin by drawing the value stream construct in the center of the page. Using the entity model as an initial starting point, copy all of the inputs and outputs associated with your selected value stream on to the environment model page. For the Order-to-Cash example, copy the *customer order request* and *customer payment* onto the environment page, along with their corresponding external entities (represented by the rounded squares with the dark edges). Refer to Figure 5.6. Continue until all of the inputs and outputs are copied.

Now you can start another workshop session to determine the additional inputs and outputs associated with this value stream. You are not talking about the whole enterprise here, just the Order-to-Cash value stream. Your workshop team composition is different and you have a smaller scope, but you still have a connection back to the whole enterprise. In this workshop session, you will start to get even more detail about the functional activities that support this value stream. Again, aggregation and decomposition are of paramount importance here too.

This early draft of Order-to-Cash needs a little discussion and you may want to review the definition of a value stream (see Chapter 3). For Widget, Inc., we chose a value stream called order to cash and another value stream called Manufacturing-to-Distribution. These choices were based on several things that are unique to Widget, Inc., and not associated with a fixed set of rules for EBA development.

1. This approach for Widget, Inc., keeps the EBA more in line with the concept of a component architecture. To reiterate, this is similar to the component architecture for a car, ship, or plane. For example, the Boeing 777 is designed to use three different engines from three different jet engine manufacturers. We want to design the EBA using the same concept.

2. This considers the possibility of outsourcing manufacturing and distribution of the widgets. Therefore, it made more sense to define two separate value streams. You can still build the EBA with this critical corporate decision pending, but before you can complete the EBA, you must have a final decision.

3. *The Great Transition*[5] also suggests separating these two value streams. Widget, Inc., is a build-to-order enterprise. We might consider a different value stream design if it were a build-to-stock enterprise or if it were a distributor. These are not absolutes, just factors that influence our value stream design decisions.

Once we have an early draft of the enterprise and the candidate value streams, we can start to make some choices with regard to the extent of the analysis we wish to undertake and how fast we want to proceed. At this point, you may choose to assign a separate team to each value stream. With an initial estimate of value streams for an enterprise, this might suggest 16 to 24 teams working concurrently. If you can pull this off, talk about throughput. More realistically, you may choose to group and assign several value streams to a single team.

You will find at this stage of the EBA that you are not limited from a critical path prospective by the approach, but by the number of teams and resources you can apply. The preferred suggestion is to give a single team responsibility for several value streams. Perhaps with this suggestion you now have four or five teams, with four to six participants each, working concurrently. This approach is an excellent balance between critical path management (time constraints) and resource utilization. Refer to Figure 5.5 for a starting point in identifying pertinent value streams.

Getting an early draft of the EBA that identifies the value streams is important not only for team assignment, but also for understanding the new structure of the enterprise. You may even want to present these

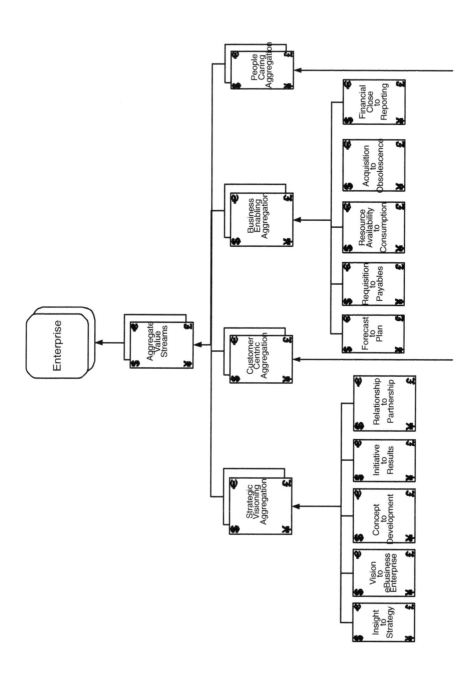

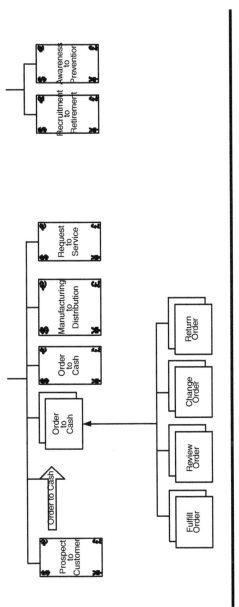

Figure 5.5 Enterprise Hierarchy Model

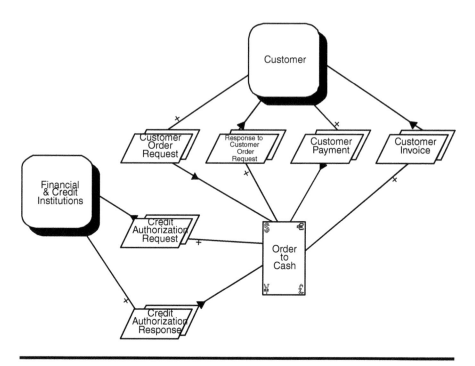

Figure 5.6 Early Draft of Order to Cash — Environment

results for review and approval before resuming development. By restructuring the enterprise according to value streams, you have a definition of what the enterprise produces and an understanding of the relationship between value streams and their external entities.

With the value stream view, you also have encapsulated the processes, activities, and tasks associated with delivering results to customers, suppliers, stakeholders, and employees, regardless of their functional origin. With this encapsulation, you have achieved some modest level of independence and can proceed with value stream development unencumbered by other teams. You still must think holistically about the enterprise, but at least at this level you can focus on a smaller unit of work — the value stream.

With an early draft of the enterprise and an early draft of each value stream, it is time to quickly review the two levels of models. Ensure that each is balanced and leveled with the other and that the sources and destinations of all inputs and outputs are also modeled. You will find that numerous balancing iterations are required throughout development of the EBA. You may also notice that you are sometimes working top-down, and at other times working bottom-up or even middle-out. This is perfectly OK. What is important is that you are thinking holistically about the enterprise and working at all levels, seeking to understand the relationships of one value stream to another. The development and nurturing of this behavior is critical to systems thinking. Any time you change an input or output to a value stream, you must analyze the impact to any other value stream.

At this time, it is preferable to get a fairly good draft of the individual value stream environment models before you start thinking about the event models and business use case models. All three of these models are critical to a complete understanding and articulation of the value stream.

- The **environment model** represents the net inputs and outputs of the value stream, connected to their respective sources and destinations, which are the external entities and other value streams. Later, when you develop the aggregate models, you will realize that the environment model is merely a copy of the infor-mation contained in the higher-level aggregate model, just broken out separately for illustrative purposes.
- The **event model** describes the events that activate the major pro-cesses within the value streams. The event model tells you what triggers the enterprise into action and what business use case is activated. These triggers in some cases suggest the types of supporting technology, for example, telephone calls, fax messages, or Internet transactions.
- The **business use case model** represents the decomposed archi-tecture of the value stream environment model. It contains the major processes or the workflow activity required to transform the inputs into outputs within the value streams. The value stream architecture model shows the relationships between the various business use cases and their respective inputs and outputs.

For posting models on the wall, we prefer to have these three models represented side by side, displayed from left to right: (1) the event model, (2) the business use case model, and (3) the environment model. It is a more logical read in this order; that is, these events trigger these processes using these inputs and outputs that are connected to their respective sources and destinations.

The environment model is the lowest level in the EBA that we use to illustrate external relationships. If you decide to maintain the connections to all sources and destinations throughout all levels of the models, you will have a maintenance nightmare and will confuse the flow of control in the workflow models. It is just too much detail that is neither valuable nor necessary. Let the encapsulation of information in the value stream work for you in this manner. If you need to understand the source or destination of an input or output, you only have to go up to the environment model level. Here again, we have a choice or compromise of conflicting requirements.

Some people argue that the information contained in these three modes is better illustrated in a single model. It is possible to combine the value stream architecture model with its sources and destinations, and you could also add the events. However, it is doubtful that you will be better able to understand and comprehend such a busy and dense model. It is almost unreadable with so much detail. Because the three peer models are inherently integrated, three separate views do not compromise your understanding, and they certainly make for easier reading.

As you analyze the EBA, you will find yourself studying this level and these three models quite frequently. You will find yourself thinking about the business use cases, the events that trigger them, and the sources and destinations of their inputs and outputs. *This level in the EBA is most effective in developing the behavior of holistic and systems thinking.* While allowing you to focus on a specific area, it still enables you to see the connection to the rest of the enterprise and its external entities.

During the early drafts of the EBA, you need to consider a few other characteristics about the value streams. Sometimes organizations and departments will attempt to influence the composition and classification of the value stream. This behavior is not necessarily intentional, but rather instinctive. We think functionally and act functionally. *Value stream behavior focuses on outputs and results, while functional behavior focuses on activities and tasks.* This is a difficult behavior to overcome. Usually functional activities are developed, controlled, and owned by organizations. Organizations or departments do not own value streams, and value streams do not own organizations or departments. For that matter, value streams do not own information repositories, transactions, or technologies. However, value streams do share organizations, departments, information repositories, transactions, and technologies.

Let us look at a relationship between a functional organization and some value streams using the following example. Widget, Inc., has a Prospect-to-Customer, an Order-to-Cash, and a Request-to-Service value stream. It also has a typical call center (a functional organization) staffed with customer service representatives (CSRs).

- The phone rings and a prospective customer requests a Widget, Inc., product catalog. In this case, the CSR is performing an instance of Prospect-to-Customer.
- On the next call, the customer places an order. In this case, the same CSR is performing an instance of Order-to-Cash.

- On the next call, a customer schedules a service call on one of Widget, Inc.'s, products. In this case, the same CSR is performing an instance of Request-to-Service.

In this example, the same CSR in the call center organization is participating in three different value streams. The same CSR is receiving the call, loading the required information into the computer systems, and building a relationship with the customer. As you can see, the value stream specifies the activities performed to achieve the desired result for the customer. *The value stream design focuses on outcomes, effectiveness, and efficiency, not on functional territories and politics.*

AGGREGATING THE VALUE STREAMS

As noted previously in the early development of the EBA, you will initially skip the two levels between the entity and the individual value streams. Even with a comprehensive set of intellectual capital, it is recommended that you skip the aggregations until you have developed a first draft of the individual value streams and their supporting hierarchy. It is very difficult to aggregate without some sort of draft of your particular value streams. Besides, the intellectual capital is merely a guide or example for reference and analysis.

How you group or classify the value streams is also important. You just cannot throw a few together randomly and expect to gain any leverage from the development teams. Of course, you will never group them based on some functional or organizational criteria, as this defeats the purpose of the value streams. It is best to group them based on who receives the value. For example, the value streams that benefit the customer belong in one group and those that benefit the employees of the enterprise in another. Some value streams benefit the stakeholders and visionary leaders of the enterprise, and others sustain and enable the operations of the enterprise.

Refer to Table 5.3 to get some suggestions for the aggregation of the value streams. Do not get too wrapped up in this initial grouping. As the EBA develops and your understanding of the enterprise matures, you may decide to adjust the groups. The more information you have, the better your choices for both value stream names and groupings. During EBA development, these adjustments will most likely occur frequently, and the development teams need to adapt their thinking as well. Changes like these, along with value stream name changes, are most certainly acceptable and typical in EBA development.

For Widget, Inc., this grouping has worked quite well. However, it is always fair to reexamine the alignment of one or two value streams. It just depends on your particular circumstances and the vision of your

Table 5.3 Value Stream Aggregates

Value Stream Aggregates	Value Streams
Customer Centric	Prospect-to-Customer Order-to-Cash Manufacturing-to-Distribution Request-to-Service
Strategic Visioning	Insight-to-Strategy Vision-to-eBusiness enterprise Concept-to-Development Initiative-to-Results Relationship-to-Partnership
Business Enabling	Forecast-to-Plan Requisition-to-Payables Resource availability-to-Consumption Acquisition-to-Obsolescence Financial close-to-Reporting
People Caring	Recruitment-to-Retirement Awareness-to-Prevention

enterprise. Use these suggestions as a starting point for your enterprise and adapt them according to your particular strategy.

You need to aggregate the individual value stream models to make them comprehensible. With 16 or more value streams, attempting to model them in a single diagram will most likely produce a model with so many crossed lines that you cannot read the model. You may find that you also need a sheet of paper the size of a large wall to draw everything so that you can read it clearly — hence the purpose of aggregation and decomposition. An aggregate model can communicate a lot of high-level information, and decomposition a lot of detail. Use aggregation and decomposition as a tool for creating understanding and insight into the EBA.

The first level below the enterprise entity is a single composite model of the four group aggregates mentioned above: customer centric, strategic visioning, business enabling, and people caring. In this level, you will see all four aggregations and their relationships with each other and the external entities defined by all of their inputs and outputs.

The second level will contain a model for each of the four group aggregates. The customer centric aggregate model, in this case, will contain four value streams — Prospect-to-Customer, Order-to-Cash, Manufacturing-to-Distribution, and Request-to-Service — and depict their relationships with each other and the external entities defined by all of their inputs and outputs. You may want to refer to Appendix D, Case Study Models, for a quick review because we will not spend any more time on these two levels.

During an engagement, you might consider focusing on the customer-centric value streams first. After all, this group should represent the true value-creating system of the enterprise and should give you the biggest bang for the buck. This does not mean that the other groups are unimportant, just that they have a different focus and are important in different ways. Again, depending on your strategic needs, your choices for analysis need to focus on the highest return on investment for the enterprise.

DETERMINING THE BUSINESS USE CASES

The business use cases are described and built in the value stream architecture models. The foundation for discovering the Order-to-Cash business use cases lies in thinking about the creation of an order and its life cycle of maintenance and reviews. This is coupled with an understanding of the events that trigger or activate the business use case. This combination provides you with the insight to develop the value stream architecture into a reasonable state of completeness. You also look at the other inputs and outputs to determine if any other business use cases are required. Herein lies another clue as to how to determine the business use cases. You focus on the inputs and outputs and build the business use case around these results. A bit later, you come back to the activities and tasks that create and consume them.

Obviously, we must receive a customer order request so that we can build, ship, and deliver the fulfilled order to the customer. During the life cycle of the order, for example, we realize that after placing the order the customer may want to review his order's status or change the quantity initially ordered. For Widget, Inc.'s, Order-to-Cash value stream, we therefore know that we need to develop the business use cases of *fulfill order, change order, review order,* and *return order.* Our business model must have these capabilities and rules that support the customer's needs.

When building the "as is" models, you probably know of several existing processes that support order fulfillment. These may provide you with a starting point for surfacing and evolving the business use cases. This knowledge, along with any documentation and intellectual capital, gives you a chance to get moving faster and establishes an early draft of the value stream architecture model. Refer to Figure 5.7 to see the value stream architecture model.

While building the Order-to-Cash value stream architecture, you may realize that the same pattern (create, retrieve, update, and delete) exists for the repository of data named *customer info* and *product configuration.* You may expect similar type business use cases in their respective value

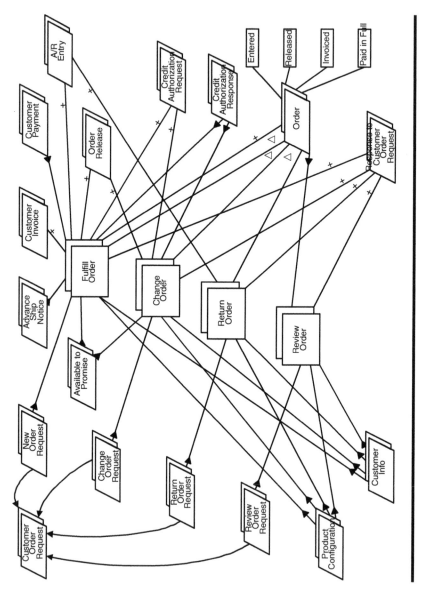

Figure 5.7 Order to Cash — Architecture

stream architectures. You have an opportunity to evaluate the other models during review sessions and to expect the same kinds of patterns, even though your expertise is in order fulfillment, not customer management. You may leverage this insight throughout the EBA. Some even refer to this create, retrieve, update, and delete process as a CRUD test. You check to see if every input and output in the value streams has a supporting activity that creates (C), retrieves (R), updates (U), and/or deletes (D) the information. These little techniques help bring the EBA to some relative state of completeness very quickly.

Some may ask, "Why is *return order* in the Order-to-Cash value stream and not in the Request-to-Service value stream? After all, the customer service center takes care of that activity." Consider these two points:

1. It is hard to break away from the thinking of "who" does the activity and assuming that this is the basis of classifying the business use cases in the value stream architectures. Remember, value streams are not owned by departments and organizations, but shared by departments and organizations.

2. You have to understand the value stream concepts, your enterprise, and your decomposition of the enterprise into value streams. Depending on your architecture, *return order* may more appropriately fit within another value stream. It is still a component in the architecture whose classification is dependent on your particular enterprise. There are no absolutes here, but rather only precedents modeled in the intellectual capital. Do not argue about points like these; just pick the best choice and continue. If you made the right choice, it will become apparent later in the EBA development. If not, revisit your decision, adapt, and continue.

To reiterate, the business use cases are architectural components within the value streams. Each is activated by a business event (trigger) that may be external or internal to the enterprise. The business use cases are workflows that transform inputs into outputs. The business use cases decompose into multiple lower levels of workflow depending on their scope and complexity.

The inputs and outputs of the business use cases may consist of both physical things and technology things. The inputs and outputs that are technology types are repositories of data, updates to these repositories of data, transactions, or messages. We will start to build some of the links to the IT architectures with technology-related inputs and outputs. For example, in the Order-to-Cash value stream architecture we find *customer info* as an input. Because we are still at a fairly high level in the EBA, *customer info* represents all of the customer-related information defined in its lexicon, as depicted in Figure 5.8.

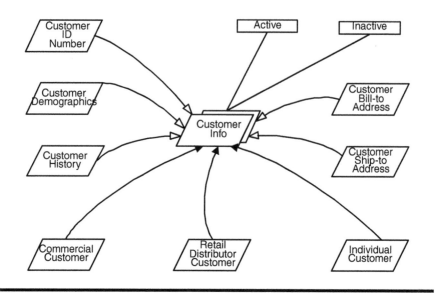

Figure 5.8 Customer Info Lexicon

We have different kinds of customers: commercial customers, retail distributors, and individual customers. Each shares or inherits properties from one another and each has a few unique characteristics. We also have different customer states, such as active and inactive. We build the lexicon in concert with the logical tables of the customer repository. This is how we maintain our link to the data/information architecture. We may reference the customer information in its entirety, or we may refer to its lower-level elements or logical tables. It just depends on what we want to represent and communicate in the model we are building.

For established data repositories, making this link is fairly simple. You just match the lexicon with the logical tables, maintaining only enough information in the lexicon to map to the entity relationship diagrams (ERD). This keeps duplication in the EBA to a minimum. When decomposing the lexicon, consider, for example, the prime keys, subtypes, and collections. For software currently under development, you will have to keep up with the analysis and design activities of their ERDs, so expect a few changes as the software evolves.

Once you have a reasonably complete draft of the value stream architecture, review all of the available models with regard to balancing and leveling the inputs and outputs. Of course, you will have to do this practically every day so that you keep the models in synchronization. Scan up and down the hierarchy of the value stream as well as across to the other value streams. With the iterative nature of EBA development, you may find it necessary to modify different parts of the model based on some discovered information or a performance improvement idea. These iterations are typical and necessary to develop a holistic model of the enterprise.

IDENTIFYING THE BUSINESS EVENTS

We capture the triggering actions affecting the business use cases in the business event models. One purpose of the event model is to assist in identifying all business use cases. In workshop sessions, you should ask the participants to try to determine all situations that will cause the enterprise to respond in a preplanned way. Remember, an event is a triggering action, not a data flow.[6] These events may also assist and lead you to the development of some very interesting high-level integration or system test cases. *If you have existing test plans for some systems, use these to start to help determine the events*, as they can be an excellent source of information.

For the *fulfill order* business use case, our first initiating external event is **customer places order**. This event can be found in Figure 5.9, which is the high-level event model for the enterprise. You may also have some variations of the high-level event such as **customer places order with a credit card** or **customer places order with cash**. Here again, we will aggregate or classify the events just as we have the business use cases. If we use the credit card example, our instantiation of *fulfill order* at some point in its processing will go into a temporary wait state while the credit card authorization is performed by an external entity. Perhaps the credit card processing is performed concurrently with some other real-time activity, but regardless, the temporary wait state will occur. It is just that in some cases, the concurrent processing will reduce the amount of time in the wait state and improve online response time.

When the external entity responds, we have another event called **financial institution responds to credit authorization request**. This event allows the instance of *fulfill order* to continue its processing. At some point, the order is accepted and released to manufacturing. In this situation the *fulfill order* business use case creates an internal event for *Manufacturing-to-Distribution* called **order released to production**. This instance of *fulfill order* goes into another wait state until manufacturing builds and distribution ships the order. Then another event called **shipping provides advanced shipping notice (ASN)** is kicked off, and later, when the temporal event **time to invoice customer** occurs, we have two internal synchronous events that trigger production of the invoice. Finally, the enterprise receives payment from the financial institution and the event **customer makes payment** again triggers the *fulfill order* business use case to completion.

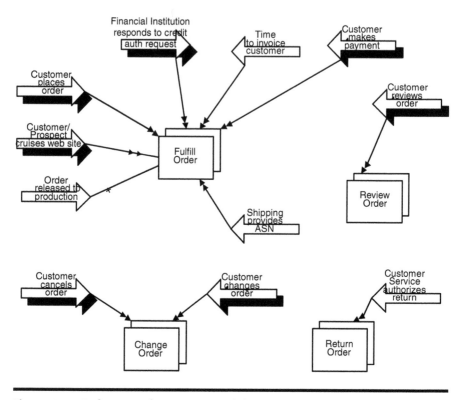

Figure 5.9 Order to Cash — Event Model

As you can see in this example, there are many variations to order processing and its supporting events. You may or may not choose concurrent processing, and you may or may not choose batch processing for invoices; nevertheless, the event model, the value stream architecture model, your existing models and documentation, and your JAD type workshop sessions seek to bring out all of the options, possibilities, and choices.

Remember, you are building logical models with defined business rules, which will provide precise requirements for the physical implementation. By using these techniques, you achieve a fuller and more complete definition of the business requirements. The user organizations more fully understand what they are requiring of both the technology and people. The IT organizations are getting a clearer description of how they will have to develop the supporting technology. By working side by side with the user organizations, they can bring to light emerging technology capabilities, which will improve performance. All of these efforts can contribute to increasing profits and building a competitive advantage for your enterprise.

Table 5.4 Order-to-Cash Event Volume Matrix

Events and Times	Midnight to 8:00 A.M.	8:00 A.M. to 4:00 P.M.	4:00 P.M. to Midnight	Total
Customer/prospect cruises Web site	4,654	55,973	41,098	101,725
Customer places order	1,274	6,832	3,386	11,492
Financial institution responds to credit authorization request	1,288	6,902	3,401	11,591
Order released to production	1,274	6,832	3,386	11,492
Shipping provides ASN	1,088	7,044	3,211	11,343
Time to invoice customer	5,922	1,029	4,332	11,283
Customer makes payment	1,448	6,644	4,101	12,193
Customer reviews order	578	3,246	1,987	5,811
Customer cancels order	34	142	77	253
Customer changes order	177	238	193	608
Customer service authorizes returns	16	48	32	96

The event models will also capture additional information, but this information can be collected more appropriately in a simple spreadsheet, as illustrated in Table 5.4. For example, we need to know the number of business events per unit of time so we can use this information to size the network and determine requisite staffing levels. We will keep this information in business terms, such as the number of orders received per hour. We can even link this statistical data back to the annual budget. For example, if we have a revenue projection, we must have a corresponding number of orders estimated to support the revenue. This enables us to size the network based on business metrics and measures linked back to the annual budget.

We can extend this approach to all value streams and for all events. Here again, we seek to more fully integrate and connect the whole enterprise rather than letting functional activities remain independent.

Systems thinking and its disciplined execution are critical to making operational use of the integrated enterprise architectures linked by the EBA. With the value stream environment, architecture, and event model, you have an excellent set of models integrated and analyzed from a holistic perspective. However, again and again you need to review the models for balancing and leveling purposes. Changes in one area will cause changes in other areas of the models. This balancing and leveling keeps the whole enterprise in synchronization.

MODELING THE WORKFLOWS

This section will only briefly cover development of the workflows because most people are very familiar with these types of models. However, we will spend some time talking about workflow decomposition and thinking about a decomposed process as a component in the architecture.

Most workflow models that exist run over multiple pages. Perhaps a few are 8 to 12 pages in length. Some are read left to right, some top to bottom, and others are just plain unreadable. On engagements, we sometimes ask who has a copy of the model, who uses the model, and where is the model kept. Once, one such model, printed on a 3-by-10-foot piece of paper, was found in a manager's desk, used by no one, and not maintained or updated. After a quick review, someone familiar with the process volunteered to explain the model, but the explanation was weak, rambling, and obviously ineffective.

How can anyone read a model of this size, much less develop supporting operational procedures or software? For those of us who have spent years in IT, remember the old spaghetti code of the 1970s and 1980s? Today we have spaghetti processes. Just as structured analysis and design methodologies brought some semblance of order out of the spaghetti code chaos in systems development, the EBA can do the same thing for spaghetti processes.

The keys to building a good workflow are insightful decomposition and strict adherence to balancing and leveling the inputs and outputs. This, coupled with a rich modeling language, enables the modeler to effectively and efficiently communicate with the reader. Building multipage workflows using quasi-standard constructs and random inputs and outputs is futile. Some say all of this modeling is too hard and a waste of time. What is hard is trying to design and code from an unclear or incomplete set of specifications, and recoding and rework are the waste of time.

For the EBA, the first-level decomposition of a business use case is a workflow. Here we have transitioned from an architecture to a workflow, not as an independent part, but as a component of a whole, the same behavior found throughout the EBA. Diagram the sequential steps of the model from left to right illustrating the transformation of inputs into outputs. The typical decomposition of a business use case may have multiple lower levels of workflows.

The first level must provide a high-level overview and understanding of the business use case. If the reader needs or wants more information, then he may choose to analyze lower levels when appropriate. By using decomposition in this manner, you prevent the spaghetti process from developing. Effective decomposition will manage the number of constructs per page such that the model is manageable, readable, and comprehensible. Each level of decomposition provides more detail and specifics about the process until the bottom of the decomposed model is reached. At this level, you are looking at the most elementary tasks performed by people, software, and the collaboration between the two.

For example, one fellow consultant was stuck on one of those 12-page spaghetti processes. He was unable to walk through the model because the off-page connectors were bouncing him all over the 12 pages. His workflow was coming up for review shortly and he felt a client sign-off was impossible. His next concern was representing the relationships to other pre- and postprocesses in the architecture and later configuring the enterprise resource planning (ERP) software from the model. On our recommendation of using a decomposition approach, it took him a day or so to completely reorganize the model from its original format into a three-level decomposed model, balanced with all inputs and outputs. His decomposition of the model created an understanding in the client's mind, and the balanced inputs and outputs illustrated the connections to other workflows. The client team acknowledged that the decomposed models were easier to read and understand. Consequently, he successfully completed the review and obtained approval of his workflow.

Refer to Figure 5.10, which is an example of the first level of decomposition of the business use case, *fulfill order*. There are six operations at this level starting with **select item from catalog** through to **post customer payment**, with their corresponding inputs and outputs. Each of these operations is an aggregate of other lower-level processes. You can consider each operation as a component in the enterprise architecture. The fact that this example has six operations is unique to Widget, Inc., and its operational environment. For a different type of manufacturing company, you might have four or seven operations at this level. It just depends on your situation and business requirements.

Some very important information is displayed at this level of the model. For example, we can determine when an instance of *fulfill order* goes into a wait state. It may also go into a wait state at a lower level, so we need to review all levels of the model before we begin our wait state analysis. This is a key process improvement imperative, eliminating or reducing wait states. We can also determine the states of an order during its life cycle by referring to the state construct. We can see that the initial order state is **entered** and its final state is **paid in full**.

There are things that we can and cannot do at this level. We can get a high-level understanding of the business use case and we can remain integrated and connected to the rest of the enterprise. But we cannot start developing UML artifacts or configuring packaged software. To get to the UML or packaged software, we will have to do one of two things: continue with the decomposition in this format until we can build UML artifacts or configure packaged software, or transition to the format of the downwind

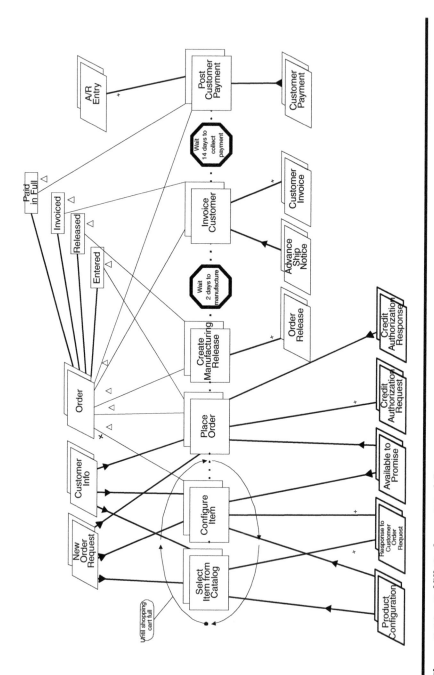

Figure 5.10 Fulfill Order — Workflow

IT domain that better suits that particular environment. Both of these options are acceptable and consistent with the concept of integrated enterprise architectures. You may even transition to a textual specification if that makes sense. Use the graphical models and text to complement one another.

Remember, we have to unify all components into a harmonious whole. You may encounter differences when you cross over into the next IT domain, but this is expected. You may also discover process improvements, emerging technologies, and ways to exploit the capabilities of the packaged software, and even improve the performance of the value stream and its supporting functional activities. This is great. It gives each participating team another chance to build that competitive advantage.

Modeling a business use case from a value stream perspective is far more logical than modeling a collection of functional activities. For example, verifying a commercial customer's credit worthiness and current "open-to-buy limits" are different functional activities that are usually performed by the same functional organization. From a functional perspective, you may model these two workflows unaware of the various other activities that occur in an operational environment. From this functional perspective, you have a parts view not a value stream view.

However, if you have the workflows modeled from the value stream perspective, you inherently have the integration and connectivity of all functional activities identified. You may then choose to take these functional activities from the value stream view and associate them with functional organizations. This is certainly acceptable, because you are simply classifying component parts out of an operational whole. From this operational whole, you can build the business function/process model as this represents the decomposition of the whole from connected parts. Conversely, you cannot logically build the value streams from the business function/process model because the parts were not initially connected as a whole.

It is imperative that you keep the models balanced between workflow levels and the rest of the EBA. When you discover the need for an additional input or output from another value stream or external entity, you must update the rest of the models affected. This is a simple skill, but a hard discipline to maintain. As you gain experience with the EBA, this behavior will occur naturally and normally. As you review other models looking for performance improvements, you will find yourself necessarily thinking about the enterprise from a holistic perspective. Consequently, your analysis will include researching the causes and effects of improvement ideas from an enterprisewide perspective. This systems thinking is a learned behavior that requires discipline and nurturing.

There are other benefits to having the balanced and leveled workflows of the business use case. Obviously, the value streams are composed of several functional activities. You may use the models to develop integration, system, or user acceptance test cases. As you may have guessed, these test cases will "compile the enterprise" to ensure the integrity, completeness, and clarity of the business rules and requirements. Then you may reuse these test cases once the software is ready for testing. It is even a good idea to have both the business and IT representatives participate in the test case development. Here again, the synergy between the two will yield positive outcomes and result in less rework in the later stages of the systems life cycle.

THE LINKS TO UML AND RUP

If you are developing object-oriented software using UML and RUP, you need to develop several software artifacts. For example, you at least need the class diagrams, activity diagrams, sequence diagrams, collaboration diagrams, and state transition diagrams. The EBA must link to UML/RUP for us to have a fully integrated model.

The various inputs and outputs described in the lexicons give us insights to the objects in the class diagram. Of course, some inputs and outputs are merely transactions or messages, and others are repositories of information. You can build the activity diagram directly from the workflow, and in a similar fashion, the sequence diagram and later the collaboration diagram. As for the state transition diagram, you may have to look at several workflows to understand all of the states of an object and the business rules and conditions for changing state. Just think: You can get all of this information out of a graphical model rather than parsing through some Victorian novel of functional specifications subject to interpretation.

Functional specifications and business activities can get very complex and full of variation. Organizing, connecting, integrating, and modeling them are more appropriately accomplished with a workflow than with a use case. One workflow can generate multiple use cases and the use case can assist in accounting for all business possibilities. It is even suggested in *Enterprise Modeling with UML*[7] that it is usually not appropriate to model workflow with use cases.

The transition to the IT domain of objects is not a one-way street, but quite the opposite. It is designed as a two-way street to surface additional IT performance improvements, as well as clarity and completeness of business requirements. If you cannot compile the business model of the enterprise, you can safely bet that you cannot compile the software either. This integration approach allows us to continuously improve and enhance the business model based on performance expectations rather than political preferences. This feedback loop is another one of those behavioral issues that require discipline and rigor. Once an improvement is discovered, you must propagate all associated changes throughout the EBA. This is sometimes a thankless but necessary task.

THE LINKS TO PACKAGED SOFTWARE

If you are using packaged software, you need to consider taking advantage of its inherent capabilities, rather than configuring the packaged software to your enterprise's old functional processes. In development of the "as is" models, keep them at a high level and with just enough detail to understand problems, opportunities, and inefficiencies. In the "to be" models, start with the packaged software flows and do minor tweaks. Seek out the optimization of the packaged software's best practices. If the packaged software workflow is cumbersome, inefficient, and unsuited to your enterprise's needs, then reconsider using it.

The transition to the IT domain of packaged software is not a one-way street either. The same feedback mechanism to the EBA is necessary to build a high-performance enterprise using the software and any other technology infrastructure. Regardless of which IT domain you transition to, the rigor and discipline of keeping the EBA fully integrated is a challenging task. But then again, this is one of the advantages of applying systems thinking to your enterprise.

You may already have several different packaged software applications from something on the Web to something on the mainframe. To model and understand the integration between all packaged software and embedded software, you must have a fully integrated model. More than likely, each packaged software product has a different modeling approach and notation. So which do you choose to model the entire enterprise? Answering this question will stimulate a great deal of debate and a few arguments, especially among consultants. "My packaged software is better than your packaged software," or maybe it is "more important," but to whom?

There is no need to have these conflicting or disruptive discussions. The EBA approach described in this book is not biased toward one package or another, but focused on the integration aspects of the enterprise, not its politics or biases. Have the EBA sit on top of all of the packaged software products, the embedded legacy applications, and all of the new and emerging Web software. Accept the fact that all of these different IT domains will have differences now and in the future. Each of these IT domains addresses a different operational or functional area of the enterprise. Each is some kind of part or component of the enterprise, so it is extremely difficult and unwise to take a part and inflict its discipline and approach on the whole.

With a fully integrated EBA, you may dispense with these types of arguments and discussions. The decision is already made. You will simply update the EBA, maintain its links and relationships throughout the model, and continue to use the EBA for performance improvement analysis. You integrate the various packaged software components into the EBA's approach and then move on to the next initiative.

THE LINKS TO PROCESS IMPROVEMENT INITIATIVES

If you are conducting a process improvement or business process reengineering initiative, the EBA is the source of your analysis and provides the insight into performance improvements. Frequently, these initiatives require some sort of software development or enhancement support. Just think, you have a set of models for conducting process analysis of the current situation, and when you finally develop the new process improvements, you use the very same models to develop software or configure packaged software. Everything is already integrated and connected to the whole, as this is the purpose of the EBA.

You may even want to run some simulations of the new processes to test and predict the results of the new improvements. Because you have the inputs and outputs modeled along with the events, most of the information required by a simulation product or tool is already located in the EBA. You even have the "wait states" modeled in the lower-level activity models. As you can see, the EBA serves as the single repository of enterprise information required by most strategic initiatives.

RATIONALIZE AND RECONCILE

Throughout development of the EBA you will have to balance and level the inputs and outputs of each model. You may find yourself splitting, merging, decomposing, and aggregating quite frequently during the early stages of the EBA. As the model grows in both breadth and depth, any modifications will require careful impact analysis. This is the heart of systems and holistic thinking. You have to understand the impact of your performance enhancements or process improvements on the whole enterprise. One client referred to this activity as rationalization and reconciliation of the EBA. This approach is iterative and evolutionary in nature, adapting to the insight and understanding gleaned from systems thinking. The initial development of the EBA is "boot camp" for its participants. It teaches them to look at the consequences of their decisions and recommendations based on a holistic view of the enterprise, in all four business dimensions.

If you want to achieve higher levels of customer satisfaction, improvements in productivity, increased profits, greater cost savings, and better decision making, you have to have an enterprisewide understanding throughout your company. You cannot confine this understanding exclusively to executives, senior managers, and key employees. You have to make it available to all employees with the expectation that every significant decision is rationalized and reconciled with the whole enterprise. The causes and effects of these decisions require predictable results in line with the strategy, goals, and objectives of the enterprise. The days of confining your thinking within the vertical walls of a functional silo are history.

REFERENCES

1. James Martin, *The Great Transition: Using the Seven Disciplines of Enterprise Engineering to Align People, Technology, and Strategy* (New York: American Management Association, 1995), Chapter 7.
2. Michael Hammer and James Champy, *Reengineering the Corporation: A Manifesto for Business Revolution* (New York: Harper Business, 1993), 118.
3. Joel Arthur Barker, *Future Edge* (New York: William Morrow, 1992), 57–58.
4. Martin, *The Great Transition*, Chapter 7, 103–107.
5. Ibid., 107.
6. Tom Demarco, *Structured Analysis and System Specification* (Englewood Cliffs, NJ: Prentice Hall, 1979), 54 (foreword by P.J. Plauger).
7. Chris Marshall, *Enterprise Modeling with UML: Designing Successful Software through Business Analysis* (Reading, MA: Addison-Wesley Longman, 2000), 65.

6

A FEW WORDS ABOUT THE OTHER ARCHITECTURES

THE LINKS TO THE OTHER ENTERPRISE ARCHITECTURES

Because this book is mostly about the enterprise business architecture (EBA), we will only spend a little time talking about the other enterprise architectures. To fully cover the architectural links to the EBA with a supporting case study would require a second book focusing on bridging the enterprise architecture gap between the business and IT strategies. With this in mind, we will keep the following discussion to a minimum.

With enterprise architecture integration as the goal, you have to start with the EBA. On the other hand, if your enterprise has all of the IT architectures modeled accurately, you have some valuable input to developing the EBA. Just prepare yourself for several iterations of updates between the business and IT architectures.

The key to integration is clearly the balanced and leveled inputs and outputs of the EBA. Without these, you will severely compromise your ability to build a set of integrated enterprise architectures. Balancing and leveling the inputs and outputs is a relatively simple skill, but it requires a fierce discipline. Building the EBA requires the same kind of rigor and discipline found in people who build data models, structured analysis/design computer-aided software engineering (CASE) models, and Unified Modeling Language (UML) diagrams. When you combine this behavior with someone who is creative, innovative, and a systems thinker, great things are possible.

Hopefully, you are using some formal framework like the Zachman Framework[1] to guide your enterprise architecture integration. As you have already seen and will continue to see, the integration techniques of the EBA are an engineering approach that enables you to connect and link specific cells of the Zachman Framework. The links are possible with the inputs and outputs found in the EBA. The links between the cells are quite formal and not loosely associated components conveniently placed next to one another.

In the following section, we will briefly describe the links to the other architectures. These are links and not replacements of artifacts normally built in other architectures. No part of the EBA is intended to displace a different model in the other architectures. Regardless of how important we feel the information technology (IT) is, or how much automation is employed from our enabling technologies, we still have to understand the collaboration between the people, processes, and technologies. This is the purpose of the EBA and the reason for its extensive use by business people in all aspects of corporate operations. Figure 6.1 is a more detailed view of the EBA models and their levels of decomposition. Review this illustration to get an overall picture of the integrated models of the EBA before we begin to discuss the IT architecture integration.

Enterprise Business Architecture to Data/Information Architecture Links

These links are the technology-related inputs and outputs, and they are described using the appropriate Enterprise Business Architecture — Modeling Language (EBA-ML) constructs. As previously mentioned, you may map the lexicons to the databases, their logical tables, a message between software components, or a standard transaction format between network tiers. One must find the full description of the technology-related inputs and outputs in the appropriate IT domain, with only a high-level representation found in the EBA lexicons. This keeps the duplication and maintenance activities to a minimum. This mapping may sound simple, but it will require a reasonably good understanding of the supporting IT documentation.

As the models are decomposed, it will be necessary to update the input and output lexicons. It is necessary to keep them in synchronization with the lexicons that are linked to the data/information architecture. Once this has been accomplished, another integration capability develops. With all of the inputs and outputs described with, for example, a **create** or **retrieve** construct, a CRUD (create, retrieve, update, and delete) matrix can be built if it is important to your project and methodology.

Enterprise Business Architecture to Application Architecture Links

The links here are all technology-related inputs and outputs and those physically related inputs and outputs produced and consumed by a logical

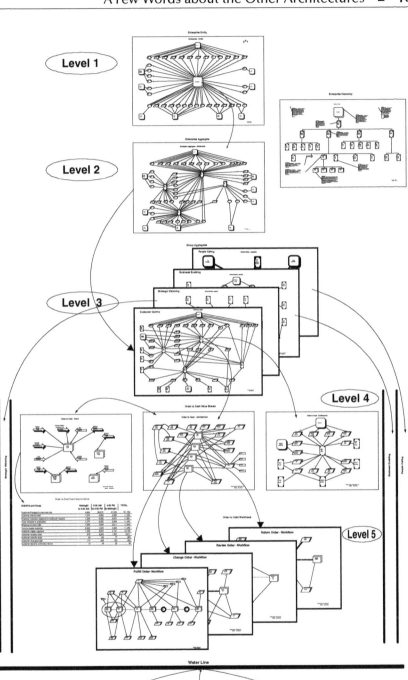

Figure 6.1 Enterprise Business Architecture Example

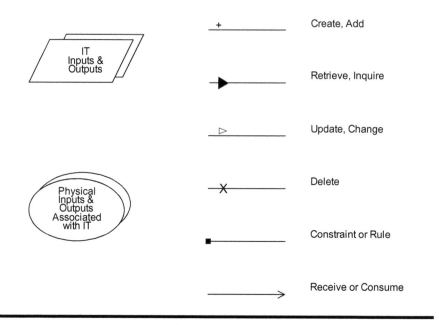

Figure 6.2 Inputs, Outputs, and Connectors

software component with their connecting constructs such as **create** and
retrieve. This architecture development will require the determination of
the relationships between the inputs and outputs and their respective
logical software components. For each value stream, you have to map
each logical software component with its associated inputs and outputs,
and you will have a corresponding application architecture. Hence, 16
value streams yields 16 value stream application architecture models.

The inputs, outputs, and their connecting constructs (such as **create**
and **retrieve**) enable you to start building the application architecture for
each value stream. At this point, you have to determine which of your
logical software components, such as order management, scheduling, and
accounts receivable, actually **create**, **update**, or **delete** the outputs, and
which ones **retrieve** the inputs. By keeping the models balanced and
leveled, and by using a rich modeling language, you can develop the
logical application architecture out of the business architecture. You will
look for the constructs found in Figure 6.2.

A logical software component may exist as a generally accepted
functional entity such as *order entry* or *accounts receivable*. You may
decide to decompose or aggregate the functional entities into additional
levels; it is your choice. The major enterprise resource planning (ERP)
packages have these generally accepted functional entities as components
in their inventory. Additionally, some have customer relationship management (CRM) and supply chain management (SCM) software as well.

The EBA models are organized according to value streams, but you may want to reorganize the application architecture models into the functional groupings suggested in Figure 3.3. You have all of the data available, but you have to restructure the 16 value stream architectures into, for this example, 8 functional application architectures to match the 8 functional groupings in the matrix. You create 8 functional application architecture models by extracting their respective logical software components with their inputs and outputs out of the 16 value stream application architecture models. Essentially, you are disaggregating the 16 models into their lowest-level elements and then reaggregating them into the 8 functional application architecture models. The same information is depicted, initially according to value stream, and later organized according to your functional groupings. You are not creating or deleting any information, just consolidating it differently.

A logical software component may also exist as an object-oriented entity. Here again, you may classify these object-oriented components into lower-level or higher-level entities, as was done in the functional example. You may even mix the functional and object-oriented components. Remember, we are building a component architecture. The fact that it is classified as a functional component or object-oriented component is not as critical as the fact that it conforms to the concepts of open systems and architectures.

Enterprise Business Architecture to Network/Technology Architecture

The links here are based on the logical software components, their logical data/information requirements, the event model, the event model volume statistics, and the logical location model.

The logical location model (or conceptual location[2]) was not discussed, but its concept is quite simple. If your enterprise has five manufacturing plants in five different locations that are structured the same way, then it has one logical location representing the five different physical locations. If your enterprise has 40 field sales offices structured the same way, then it has one logical field sales office. The objective here is to get to a common understanding of the kind of logical connectivity we need between the logical locations and their enabling IT. The event model helps us here, and the event model volume statistics provide us with capacity requirements driven by business volumes.

From the logical location model, you determine the required access to the various logical software components (with their logical data/information). The event model helps you determine this access. The event initiates a business use case that requires access to several logical software components. You now know what you have to connect to in order to deliver the required results. The event model volume statistics help you select the most cost-effective network connection. For example, very low volume Web access occasionally throughout the day may be satisfied with a dial-up connection. Extremely high volume access may require a Digital Subscriber Line (DSL) connection.

Here again, you will have a logical connectivity model for each value stream or 16 of them. If you have 9 logical locations, then you will have to disaggregate the 16 into their lowest-level elements, and then reaggregate them into the 10 logical location models. You did a similar exercise for the application architecture. You simply changed the organization of information from a value stream view into a logical location view. Again, you did not create or delete any information, but you did consolidate it differently.

Enterprise Business Architecture to Security Architecture

The integration is based on determining the security functional activities dictated by corporate policy. You may define the security functional activities as rules or constraints in the value streams and extract them out for security planning. Most of the input to the security architecture is based on the integration of the data/information, application, and network/technology architectures, but we must identify physical access as well. For every connection, for every application use, for every data access, we need to evaluate the need for authentication and authorization. From the network/technology architecture, you may determine the logical security requirements and placement across the network.

Enterprise Business Architecture to Organizational Architecture

We built logical software components, either functional or object oriented, as described earlier. The collaborations between people and IT, and the activities that will remain manual, require analysis for the organizational architecture. Here again, we will classify or aggregate these activities based on our organizational objectives. This classification or aggregation is similar in concept to what we did with the logical software components, except these are people type activities. Instead of classifying these people type activities under some logical software component hierarchy, we will classify them under an organizational hierarchy. You may classify them along the traditional lines of a functional hierarchy or perhaps along a process hierarchy; it is your choice.

This very brief overview illustrates the integration aspect of the aforementioned architectures. Each architecture is logical in that its physical implementation is not necessarily known. The logical nature of the architectures has the added benefit of allowing for change and flexibility at the more detailed level without constantly impacting the high-level structure of the overall EBA. However, as we all know, we can start to sense the physical designs as the models mature and integration gets tighter. Hopefully, with this holistic view of the enterprise, we can apply some sound systems thinking for selecting and implementing the enabling IT. As we develop crafted software, configure packaged software, and select network devices, we may have to update the models accordingly. In this case, the models may become a little more physical in nature. This is acceptable as long as we keep to the spirit and intent of logical modeling.

The ability to derive, deduce, link, and integrate one model with another is somewhat empirical in nature and certainly not mechanical. To derive one of these downwind models from the upwind model or models demands a thorough understanding of the downwind model's requirements and integration needs. The key technique applied in this approach is judicious management of the inputs and outputs from the EBA. After all, the inputs and outputs allow you to focus on *what* you are producing in the value streams. The inputs and outputs are the clear definition of the relationships between components in the architecture or the relationships between your enterprise and its external entities. Without these balanced and leveled inputs and outputs, any attempt to integrate one model with another will fail. You have to know this information, and your effectiveness and efficiency improves if it is represented graphically.

One could take this approach and develop EBA and architecture integration supporting software, as there are enough rules and standards for software specifications. Software, however, is an inadequate replacement for sound, intuitive, systems thinking. It is excellent for automation and storage, but no substitute for serious research and analysis. You cannot learn systems thinking from software. You have to get out and do the manual balancing and leveling and perform cause-and-effect analysis or you just will not get it. Systems and holistic thinking are learned behaviors, characteristic of visionaries, sometimes stimulated from instinctive business foresight or a serious threat to corporate survival. When developing the EBA, you must maintain a customer-centric focus and ultimately improve enterprise performance. Waiting or searching for software that will do this for you is futile.

These last few paragraphs illustrate the hardwiring capability of the EBA. Out of the logical enterprise business architecture comes the other remaining logical architectures. Thus, we truly have integrated the enterprise architectures. Just remember, the strategic objectives are connected to the value streams, and therefore, everything is aligned and connected in the EBA. As you can probably see, it is a modest skill but a demanding behavior. This systems thinking is tough, but with a rigorous and disciplined approach it is achievable.

INTEGRATING THE EBA USING A SOFTWARE PRODUCT

Integrating the architectures of the enterprise is a very demanding and detailed undertaking. The illustrations presented in this text used Visio® as the modeling tool, which is inexpensively accessible to almost every enterprise. You can review the linking capabilities in Appendix D. However, many enterprises will prefer a more sophisticated modeling tool. There are several very good modeling tools on the market, and most follow the Zachman Framework.[3] Your organization should consider both the low-tech option with Visio and the high-tech option with a commercial enterprise architecture (EA) modeling tool. Carefully consider the needs of your enterprise and use a formal approach[4] for selecting the modeling tool for your organization.

Perhaps you should consider Visio first to get an understanding of the integration concepts and requirements. Maybe you will consider this as a pilot project or learning project before moving on to a commercial EA modeling tool. Do not run off and buy the first EA tool you find, but carefully research each vendor's capabilities and future enhancements. Then, with the experience gleaned from your pilot project, you can map your requirements to the tool's features.

We did some research into one vendor's product and were pleased to find that it could capture and depict the same connectivity described with the EBA, both up to the strategy and down to the enabling IT. We were also told that adding a new notation to accommodate the EBA we have been discussing was doable and not a major undertaking, as the EA tool was designed to adapt to new notations and capabilities without extensive software modifications. Most likely, all of the EA tool vendors are building this type of capability. Just remember to have a thorough understanding of your modeling needs and the EBA concepts before selecting a commercially available EA tool.

REFERENCES

1. John A. Zachman, *The Zachman Framework*, http://www.zifa.com.
2. Steven H. Sepwak and Steven C. Hill, *Enterprise Architecture Planning: Developing a Blueprint for Data, Applications and Technology* (Wellesley, MA: QED Publishing Group, 1993), 228.
3. Zachman, *The Zachman Framework*.
4. David Rudiwitz, "Selection of Enterprise Architecture Tools: A Primer for How and Why," 2003, http://www.antevorte.com/news.htm.

III

NEXT STEPS

7

WHERE DO WE GO FROM HERE?

WHAT CAN YOU EXPECT FROM YOUR INITIAL ARCHITECTURAL DEVELOPMENT?

You want to set some realistic expectations from the results of your enterprise business architecture (EBA) development. However, we need to define a few more terms to help in the understanding and explanation. The development of the EBA is characterized in two areas. The first is relative to the enterprise or business unit as a whole, and the second is relative to the value streams.

Development of the EBA Relative to the Enterprise or Business Unit

As previously stated, you do not have to model all of the value streams concurrently, following the same schedule of development. Based on your strategic priorities, you may choose one of the aggregates of value streams or possibly a handful of value streams that you are particularly interested in. This is perfectly OK, but you must at least identify all of the value streams to have a fairly complete enterprise structure. In the metaphor of your home, adding that sunroom, patio, and pool will cause you to carefully consider the area of construction that touches and extends the existing architecture of your house. However, the rooms and other unaffected areas will have minimum impact on the home improvements, and it may not be necessary to depict them in any great detail.

When planning to develop and implement an EBA, the enterprise must consider the evolutionary nature of the enterprise itself, its models, and the structured EBA approach. Developing the current or "as is" EBA down

Table 7.1 Enterprise Development States

Development State	Description	Capabilities
Enterprise modeled at high level	All enterprise value streams identified, approved, modeled, balanced, and leveled down through the value stream environment level with the event and architecture models	Provides information for enterprise strategic planning Provides information for enterprise engineering
Enterprise modeled at midlevel	All enterprise value streams modeled, balanced, and leveled down through the first level of workflow for each business use case	Provides information for value stream reinvention

to midlevel for each value stream takes time, at least several months (depending on the amount of intellectual capital and human resources you have on hand) for an enterprise or self-contained business unit. It must proceed in an orderly fashion, initially from top to bottom, or from the entity down to the value streams.

Once the enterprise is modeled down through this midlevel, then value stream decomposition may proceed from an integrated and holistic perspective. Refer to Table 7.1 and Table 7.2 for the EBA development states. It is not necessary to "slam dunk" the whole enterprise through the process of developing the models all at one time. Rather, once the midlevel enterprise models are developed (representing the breadth of the enterprise), then the development of individual value streams may commence (representing the depth of the enterprise). This enables the enterprise to focus on priority initiatives and the supporting value streams, and not just on some arbitrary schedule based on a best guess.

Also, it is important to note that effective and efficient value stream decomposition will not occur without the whole of the enterprise modeled through at least the midlevel. Without this level of development, a value stream is too isolated and the models will be unable to connect to other identified enterprise value streams and external entities. The analysis of proposed improvements is also hindered without recognizing the connections and consequent impact on the rest of the enterprise.

Development of the EBA Relative to the Value Stream

The first usable state of the EBA is an enterprise modeled at the high level. This means that all enterprise value streams are identified, approved,

Table 7.2   Value Stream Development States

Development State	Description	Capabilities
Value stream modeled at midlevel	A value stream modeled, balanced, and leveled down through the first level of workflow for each business use case	Provides information for value stream reinvention Provides information for procedure/process redesign Provides information for total quality management (TQM)
Value stream defined at midlevel with expectations	A value stream defined with approved metrics and measures for each business use case	Enables the linkage and alignment with the enterprise strategic plan's objectives
Value stream managed at midlevel	A value stream operational and performed on a routine basis using the models for direction and guidance for each business use case	Enables the value stream to achieve predictable and desired results with continuous improvement
Value stream modeled at low level	A value stream modeled, balanced, and leveled down through the appropriate lower level for transition to an information technology (IT) implementation for each business use case	Enables packaged software configuration or Unified Modeling Language (UML)/ Rational Unified Process (RUP) development or logical IT modeling in a software development methodology
Value stream modeled at swim lane level	A value stream modeled, balanced, and leveled down through the most elementary workflow	Enables the ability to craft software for each business use case

modeled, balanced, and leveled down through the value stream environment, event, and architectural level. You can see from Table 7.1 the associated capabilities from an EBA in this stage of development. This stage gives you a very good understanding of a fairly complete enterprise structure. By this time, you will have also gotten your EBA participants well into the behaviors of customer centric and systems thinking. From this state, you may move on to developing selected value streams for further analysis and performance improvement. This also represents the minimum level of development necessary before you may realize any value from the EBA project.

The usable state of a value stream is a value stream modeled at the midlevel. In this case, you have completed the value stream development down through level 5 of the hierarchy. Its corresponding capabilities are also described in Table 7.2.

Based on what capabilities you need from the EBA, you can determine which development state you need to reach and plan an appropriate schedule. A quick review of a typical EBA project schedule (see Appendix B) implies that it will take about a month to model the enterprise at a high level and about another month to model a single group of value streams to a midlevel. From this development state, you can review your strategic direction and decide what to develop next.

You may be wondering how to use the EBA for replacing a legacy software component with a packaged software component. For example, you are installing a new *order entry* component or a *new accounts payable* component. In this case, you need to model all value streams that share the software component down to a low level. Because value streams share logical software components, you must identify each value stream that uses the component. Your value stream and logical software component matrix (see Figure 3.3 for an example) will provide the initial insight to those value streams that will require analysis. Each will require modeling down to the activity level to fully develop the desired replacement component capabilities.

Conduct a serious review of Table 7.2, as it describes the various states of model development. Each state is described in terms of decomposition detail along with the capabilities it enables. The states are listed in sequential order of maturity. Simply put, you cannot achieve a lower state without first achieving a higher state in the table. However, several value streams may proceed through development in parallel, but on different priority schedules. The key factor is to consider development of those value streams that are most critical and important to the enterprise in terms of their contributions to success.

EBA PREPARATION AND PLANNING

Developing a schedule of tasks for project management purposes may proceed with the above understanding of the various states of EBA modeling. With the states defined and their capabilities understood, implementation plans may proceed based on the desired capabilities. As previously noted, the sequence of value stream decomposition is based on its importance and contributions to the enterprise. The speed of development is fully dependent upon the resources assigned, their experience in enterprise modeling, their industry expertise, and the number of scheduled workshops. The speed of development is also influenced by leadership's formal commitment to the EBA, assigning it a high priority, and communicating the shared goals and expectations of the EBA throughout the enterprise. Refer to Appendix B for an example of an EBA project schedule.

Most of the direction in developing the EBA is coordinated by the first-tier teams. These directors, midlevel managers, senior business analysts, and senior technicians are usually responsible for results. They receive priority, funding, approval, and resources from the executives sponsoring the EBA initiative. The second-tier teams are usually individuals who actually perform the tasks described in the workflows and provide the detailed information required to build the models. The high-level implementation activities required to develop the models into the desired state are described in Table 7.3.

Assuming you follow the EBA approach and concepts, you can also expect to see performance improvements from the implementation of your strategic initiatives. You will need some valid historical performance statistics from prior activities to fairly and objectively assess the return on investment. Without this historical data, any assessment will have some level of subjectivity applied and possibly compromise the results.

GETTING PAST MANAGEMENT BUREAUCRACY AND FINDING VISIONARY LEADERSHIP

The EBA provides a graphical representation of the shared knowledge of the enterprise. It comes out of people's heads and text-based manuals, is documented in a model, and is then initially posted on a wall and later perhaps on the Web. Be forewarned that the wall area may extend as much as 80 linear feet in length.

However, the decomposition approach for both the processes and data enables the analysis of the key relationships and most important inputs and outputs. Keeping the models balanced and leveled gives you the holistic view of the enterprise by getting you to look across the enterprise to understand the numerous relationships between processes. This, coupled with the appropriate metrics and measures found in a sound strategy, allows you to analyze a new initiative relative to its impact on the whole enterprise, not just a few functional departments. It enables you to understand how the initiative will impact the customer or possibly a stakeholder and to determine the true value delivered to the enterprise.

Table 7.3   EBA Implementation Activities

Development State	Implementation Activities
Enterprise modeled at high level	Train executives and first-tier teams in value stream concepts Train executives and first-tier teams in modeling concepts Build models through facilitated workshops Present and review models with enterprise strategists
Enterprise modeled at midlevel	Train second-tier teams in value stream concepts Train second-tier teams in modeling concepts Build models through facilitated workshops Present and approve models with managers
Value stream modeled at midlevel	Train second-tier teams in value stream concepts Train second-tier teams in modeling concepts Build models through facilitated workshops Present and approve models with managers Use models for value stream execution
Value stream defined at midlevel with expectations	Use models for value stream analysis
Value stream managed at midlevel	Use models to develop schedules and track projects Use project results for reward and recognition Use results for value stream analysis
Value stream modeled at low level	Train all teams in value stream concepts Train all teams in modeling concepts Use models as specifications and requirements for software implementation using most any software development methodology Use models for training operational personnel
Value stream modeled at swim lane level	Use models as specifications and requirements for crafted software development

Having understood these points, ask a manager to initiate this project and do not forget to request the 80 feet of wall space. Most likely, you will get several variations of a negative answer. The following are typical responses:

- My boss hasn't told me to look into this kind of activity.
- Everybody is too busy working on other things.
- It will take too much time and too many resources.
- I am too busy with projects already in trouble and firefighting daily problems.
- We don't have these of problems, so why do we need this solution?
- It will cost too much (I only have enough in my budget to redo current initiatives if necessary).
- It doesn't have supporting software.
- That's for the business guys and we only do technology things.
- I don't see any reason to change, as we are eventually getting the work done anyway.
- This is neither an accepted nor approved approach in our organization.
- That is not the way we do things around here.

Perhaps the manager will attempt to create some sort of fear out of doing this kind of project. After all, if you do not immediately fight some particular fire, the organization will collapse. And when it collapses, you will get the blame for diverting your attention away from the fires. The future is a scary and risky place, unknown and undefined, whereas today is full of firefights, but comfortable. The future is an undiscovered country, a new paradigm with a completely different set of rules, rules that you get to write.

So do not ask a manager; ask a visionary leader. Ask someone who dares to look into the future, someone intimate with the corporate strategy, someone with a customer-centric view, and someone whose career goals are aligned with the enterprise's goals. Stay away from managers who have sold out to the organizational fiefdoms. Find those visionary leaders who have bought in to the success of the whole enterprise and the use of the EBA to achieve predictable results. After all, this is a corporatewide initiative. You have to have the cooperation of the entire enterprise (or business unit) to build, implement, and make the EBA operational. Strategic planning, business alignment, performance improvement, and integrated enterprise architecture analysis are not yearly one-time projects, but a way of corporate life. You do not start planning for your children's education when they turn 15 or 18, but during their formative years, and hopefully for the rest of their lives. We need the same kind of interest and commitment for the enterprise.

THE POWER OF ARCHITECTURES

Today, enterprises must adapt and adapt quickly. How and when you adapt requires a thorough analysis of the marketplace and its opportunities.

A living strategy provides you with these keen insights and measurements of success. With value streams based on results and contributions, aligned with the strategic objectives and initiatives, you remain focused on the goals constantly in your sights. By placing the customer above all functional silos and personal fiefdoms, you keep the enterprise priorities fixed on the profit and revenue-generating sources.

With all the major enterprise architectures integrated, articulated in a common language, and understood by all corporate employees, you have a compelling force for change. You have a framework of models that are integrated, comprehensible, and useful. You can decompose your component architecture for detailed analysis, performance improvement, or outsourcing determination. And finally, with a *strategy-to-results* approach, you can verify and trace all business requirements throughout the analysis, design, and implementation phases, and then measure the operational impact on the whole enterprise.

Each strategic initiative undertaken to improve performance requires a serious project plan. The first steps of that plan may simply take the "pulse and temperature" of the current situation or build stability into the current situation. Once stabilized, understood, and analyzed, you can then predict the outcomes and results of the strategic initiatives. These are realistic and achievable expectations supported by your EBA, not some seat-of-the-pants guess by some pompous or boastful manager. These managers are really just spectators in the grandstands pointing out every player's flaws and shortcomings and do not really produce anything of value. Leaders are part of the solution if they are in the arena and are committed to the strategic EBA initiative.

You do not need a miracle to do this — just visionary leadership and a committed decision to do it, and then get on with it. Most of the architectures discussed are well understood, but not properly formatted and integrated. The integration and architecture skills are learnable. In reality, it is a behavioral issue, requiring more insight, discipline, and rigor rather than skill. Most of the integration and architecture skills are mechanical and are capable of evolving into software. However, we do not yet have software available that does our thinking for us.

That is why we need the strategy, vision, corporate objectives, and enterprise initiatives normally found in a sound strategic plan. This strategic plan, coupled with a well-defined set of integrated enterprise architectures, provides the superior insight, unity of purpose, and synergy for achieving breakthrough results. Remember, the key enabler in the 21st century is architecture, architecture, architecture. It gives us a chance to get out in front of the pack and lead for a while. Instead of having a strategic plan simply focused on catching up with the competition, we cause the competition to react or catch up with us. When they finally catch up, we have moved ahead again, and the competition is left behind. We, on the other hand, are constantly evolving, adapting, and changing toward our exciting new strategy.

This commitment will require several dedicated resources and approximately four months to set up, organize, and implement. Ongoing support is also required until the behavior modifications and supporting activities evolve into the norm. Critical to successful implementation is an honest change in behavior away from leading the enterprise from an organization's or product's view toward leading the enterprise from the customer's view. This change management is essential to the success of the implementation. Also, splitting team members' time between multiple major initiatives, rather than focusing wholly on the task at hand, may jeopardize the success of the endeavor. And, of course, it needs the unyielding support of leadership from the top.

8

CONCLUSION

Having fulfilled the requisite enterprise modeling needs and using the enterprise business architecture (EBA) models developed to understand the enterprise, implementation of prioritized strategic initiatives may begin. In addition to providing boundaries, the integrated enterprise models represent the common repository of data, information, and knowledge about the enterprise. The graphical representations precisely describe the enterprise in clear and understandable terms. The scope of the models is also four-dimensional, considering functional activities within a department, cross-functional activities within the company, customer and supplier activities, and competitor activities such as time to market. This holistic view and understanding enables information technology (IT) alignment with enterprise objectives, goals, and strategies as well.

It is from these models that the current state of the enterprise is analyzed, and the IT architectures, frameworks, and transition plan to the future state are developed. The models also allow decomposition of the enterprise into manageable and understandable units, thereby reducing complexity. It is from this decomposition that effectiveness, efficiency, and adaptability are designed, engineered, and optimized by the enterprise. However, it must be understood that no single model or decomposed unit provides the "silver bullet" solution for the enterprise. The synthesis of information from the integrated business and IT models provides numerous links, which unite the enterprise into a holistic entity, thereby aligning a complete enterprise strategy with people, processes, and technology.

In giving definition and structure to the enterprise, it is a basic tenet that no complex system is optimum to all parties concerned and has all functions optimized. Consequently, architecting, or the development of an architecture or framework to control and delimit complexity, is a matter of fit, balance, and compromise of many factors and many interests. This is especially true in the development of a structure, or architecture, within which are built complex IT systems that will support and enable the business of the enterprise.

A system is considered a set of different elements connected or related in such a fashion as to perform a unique function not performed by the elements alone: a gestalt. The most important and distinguishing characteristic of a system, therefore, is the relationship among the elements. The definition of a system can be further refined and broken into two basic parts:

- A system is a complex set of dissimilar elements or parts so connected or related as to form an organic whole.
- The whole is greater than the sum of the parts; that is, the system has properties beyond those of the individual parts. The purpose of building systems is to acquire those properties provided by the whole.

As previously mentioned, the essence of systems is relationships, interfaces, form, fit, and purpose. Therefore, the essence of architecting (and modeling) is structuring, simplification, compromise, and balance. The challenge is in the control, if not the reduction, of complexity and uncertainty, and this must be reflected in the architecture.

The development of an architecture is pragmatic as well. The architectures must expand or reduce the problem at hand to a realistic, workable, and manageable size and structure. The framework must dictate structures that are achievable. A component architecture realizes this benefit.

Experience provides the answer to why there is a need for architectures and frameworks. Enterprises with inadequate, poorly defined, and undocumented architectures are prone to high business and IT resource expenditures and have difficulty fitting system components together. That is, the pieces of a system do not fit and satisfy the intended purpose. An architecture makes the pieces fit and facilitates the integration and resolution of structural conflicts. An architecture defines the whole and the parts.

Many of these structural conflicts are blamed on the IT departments. Some companies even feel that they are held hostage by their IT organizations, unable to implement new mission-critical capabilities quickly, efficiently, and safely. The root causes of these problems are found in the lack of formal and integrated architectures of *both* the business and IT. The cumulative impact of years of short-term thinking and knee-jerk reactions to threats in the marketplace finally begins to surface with obvious consequences. We somehow feel that the current pressures of the business demand an immediate response, even at the expense of sound and rational strategic thinking — hence the "rush to chaos" experienced on a daily basis. The solution is *not* a faster approach to the next disaster, but an anticipation of the business opportunity ahead of the marketplace, founded on an adaptive architecture. We must implement proactive initiatives, not desperate, last-minute, poorly planned projects that only react to missed opportunities or threats from competitors. It is a problem that must be shared across the enterprise, not dumped in the laps of the IT department with a due date of yesterday.

Serious difficulties arise when the number and nature of elements result in so many complex interfaces that what one subsystem does to the rest is no longer as simple as single inputs and outputs. In this case, the relationships between function and form break down. The architecture, the creation of a framework or structure, brings order out of chaos, establishes system relationships, and acquires the desired properties of the whole.

As with modeling the enterprise business architecture (EBA), an IT architecture can perhaps be best understood with a top-down description of the structure of the system. Therefore, models can help in describing the structure. In this case, a model is an abstraction of what the participants think and hope the end system and its environment will look like. By implying a great deal of internal structure, a model can communicate a wealth of information in a simple aggregated form. For example, a model of a house is quickly understood by all parties, not only in its external shape, but also in its likely electrical, plumbing, and heating systems, its living space, and its relationship to its surroundings.

The best architecture is based on the complete submission of the individual parts to the purpose of the whole. "Form follows purpose" becomes a guiding principle. Successful systems can be developed following an architecture that is driven by purpose instead of form. However, it should be noted that successful architectures evolve slowly and are not created with such detail that they stifle innovation. If an architecture is overdefined, the builders will have no choice or flexibility other than to "build to print." That is, with too much specificity, the system developer or implementer will not have the option to improve or adapt the design to meet changing business environmental demands or technological changes.

To simply take what currently exists and try to make it work together in most cases is not realistic or pragmatic, nor will it meet the business needs of an organization. No builder, designer, or business engineer can remedy a fundamentally flawed concept. However, given a sound architectural foundation, success can be realized and will only be contingent on the skills of the builders, designers, and the engineers.

Finally, the enterprise business architecture models and IT architectures and frameworks without a supporting plan accomplish little or nothing, never reaching implementation. Therefore, strategic planning for both the business and IT is tantamount to success if anything is to be accomplished in an orderly, efficient, and effective manner and support the business needs of the enterprise.

For most enterprises, a missing link exists between strategy and results. At times even well-designed, fully funded initiatives seem to fall short of executive expectations. Cost overruns and frequent delays are the norm, not the exception. To prevent this, we must understand, articulate, and develop an integrated enterprise business architecture. We must understand the EBA's role in the enterprise and treat it not as an isolated component but as part of a unified whole.

Sometimes we lose our focus and get lost in the daily all-consuming crises and the firefights to resolve them, or we become befuddled in the increasing complexity of technology. In the mid-1990s, some thought we were entering a new age, an age of solutions — the e-Age, an age in which technology would answer everything. Evidence was everywhere, numerous terms and phrases were preceded by e-, such as e-business, e-enterprise, e-learning, and the like. As we now know, these new buzzwords were just fads, similar to the ones that occur in the clothing and apparel industry. This climate generated numerous e-projects, which focused on some part of the enterprise that needed e-enhancing. In the haste to embrace this trend, we then had a real crisis: declining e-profits and the corporate e-meltdowns. Many felt it was "the worst of times."

Perhaps we are entering a new age as well as a new century. However, most likely it is not the e-Age, as we had previously thought. Perhaps, though, it is the age of architecture — an age of understanding connectivity and causality; an age or mature state when integrated enterprise architectures are the new, long-term, strategic behavior and not a passing fad; an age of structure and order, one that is distant from collapse and chaos; a new era of discipline and holistic thinking. Many now feel that this is "the best of times."

The formality and discipline of the EBA may frighten some business people, and others may feel it is unnecessary. After all, an architecture including one of the business seems too structured, too engineering-like, and too technical for a businessperson. Many still prefer the informality of loosely defined diagrams and business models presented in colorful and creative presentations. However, these are mostly useless during the life cycle of a strategic initiative, because they provide little substance beyond the show and frequently fail to deliver the expected results. Besides, most managers think they can wing it, even at the risk of failure, rather than formally design and engineer success with an EBA. But their days are numbered, and a new discipline is emerging with the enterprise business architecture forging the links between corporate strategy and tangible results.

IV

APPENDICES

Appendix A

ENTERPRISE BUSINESS ARCHITECTURE — MODELING LANGUAGE (EBA-ML)

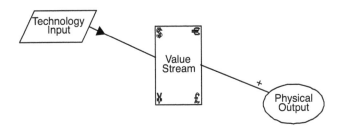

The information in this guide provides explanations for the Enterprise Business Architecture — Modeling Language (EBA-ML) (copyright © 2004) constructs. The shapes or configurations of the constructs are illustrated and defined, and many have examples. The examples are simple stand-alone illustrations, and in several cases, details such as pre- and poststeps or various inputs and outputs were not shown in order to keep the illustration easy to comprehend. For a fuller understanding, refer to the models presented in *Enterprise Business Architecture: The Formal Links between Strategy and Results* (CRC Press, 2004).

ENTERPRISE AND EXTERNAL ENTITIES

A square with rounded corners and a clear border is used to represent the *enterprise entity* or *business unit entity*. This is the enterprise or one of its business units selected for analysis and performance improvement.

A smaller square with rounded corners and a dark shadow is used to represent *external entities*. Examples of external entities are customers, suppliers, vendors, and financial institutions.

INPUTS AND OUTPUTS

An elongated circle with a clear border is used to represent an *aggregation* of *physical inputs* or *physical outputs*. There are three types of aggregations: whole/parts, shared properties, and containers. Refer to the examples in "Aggregations of Inputs/Outputs."

An elongated circle is used to represent a *physical input* or *physical output*. Generally, this input or output cannot be further decomposed without losing its identity. Refer to the examples in "Aggregations of Inputs/Outputs."

A slanted rectangle with a clear border is used to represent an *aggregation* of *technology inputs* or *technology outputs*. There are three types of aggregations: whole/parts, shared properties, and containers. Refer to the examples in "Aggregations of Inputs/Outputs."

A slanted rectangle is used to represent a *technology input* or *technology output*. Generally, this input or output cannot be further decomposed without losing its identity. Refer to the examples in "Aggregations of Inputs/Outputs."

BUSINESS PROCESSES AND TECHNOLOGY APPLICATIONS

A vertical rectangle with a clear border, containing international currency symbols in the corners, is used to represent an *aggregation* of selected *value streams* as defined by the enterprise. For example, the customer centric aggregation consists of the Prospect-to-Customer, Order-to-Cash, Manufacturing-to-Distribution, and Request-to-Service value streams.

A vertical rectangle with international currency symbols in the corners is used to represent a *value stream*. A value stream is an end-to-end collection of activities that create a result for a customer, who may be the ultimate customer or an internal end user of the value stream. The value stream has a clear goal: to satisfy or delight the customer.[1] These are the core business processes of the enterprise or business unit under analysis. For example, Order-to-Cash.

A horizontal rectangle with a clear border is used to represent a group of *aggregated business processes*. This is a higher-level representation of the group that is decomposed into lower-level business processes or activities. The inputs and outputs of the aggregated processes are balanced and leveled with the lower-level decomposed processes or activities.

A horizontal rectangle is used to represent the *lowest level* of a *business process* or *activity*. There is no further decomposition of this level.

A horizontal rectangle with a small computer type symbol in the upper left corner and a clear border is used to represent a group of *aggregated application functions*, for example, accounts receivable. This is a higher-level representation of the group that is decomposed into lower-level application functions, such as check credit limit. The inputs and outputs of the aggregated application are balanced and leveled with the lower-level decomposed application functions.

A horizontal rectangle with a small computer type symbol in the upper left corner is used to represent the *lowest level* of an *application function*. There is no further decomposition of this level.

AGGREGATIONS OF INPUTS/OUTPUTS

Whole/Part

A right-angled up arrow is used to illustrate *whole/part relationships*. You must have all of the parts to have the whole.

Example for physical inputs/outputs:

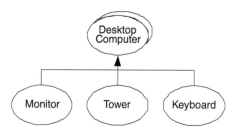

Example for technology inputs/outputs:

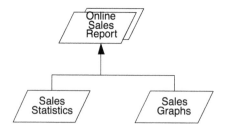

Shared Properties

A curved solid arrow arc is used to illustrate a *shared properties* relationship. These relationships share something in common or may inherit these shared properties. The shared properties are defined by the enterprise. The end with the arrow points to the higher-level element.

Example for physical inputs/outputs:

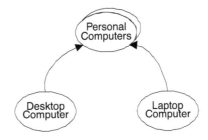

Example for technology inputs/outputs:

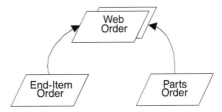

Contains

A curved open arrow arc is used to illustrate *contains relationships*. These relationships are broadly defined, and sometimes the container is composed of several dissimilar but logical elements. The relationships are defined by the enterprise. The end with the arrow points to the higher-level element.

Example for physical inputs/outputs:

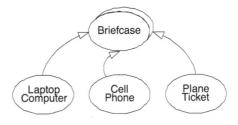

Example for technology inputs/outputs:

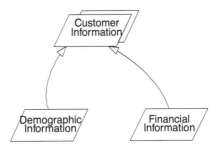

CONNECTORS FOR PROCESSES AND/OR INPUTS/OUTPUTS

Create, Add

_____ +

A line connector with a *plus sign* is used to illustrate that something is *created* or *added*. The end with the plus sign is attached to the created or added output.

Example:

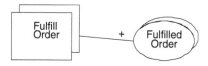

Retrieve, Inquire

————————◄

A line connector with a *solid arrowhead* is used to illustrate that data or information is *retrieved* or *inquired* by the process or activity. The end with the solid arrowhead is attached to the input accessed.

Example:

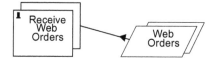

Update, Change

_____ ◁ ___

A line connector with a *delta sign* is used to illustrate that something is *updated, changed,* or somehow *modified.* The end with the open delta is attached to the output affected.

Example:

Delete

————————✕—

A line connector with an *X* is used to illustrate that something is *deleted.* The end with the *X* is attached to the output deleted.

Example:

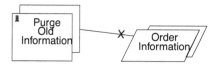

Constraint, Rule

A line connector with a *solid box* is used to illustrate that something must be used as a *constraint* or *rule*. The end with the solid box is attached to the input or output that specifies the constraint.

Example:

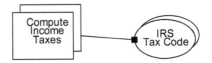

Receive or Consume

A line connector with an *arrowhead* is used to illustrate that something is *received* or *consumed* in a process or activity. The end with the arrowhead is attached to the receiving or consuming process or activity.

Example:

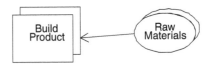

Causes

A line connector with a *double-headed arrow* is used to illustrate that something has *caused* something else to happen. The end with the double-headed arrow is attached to the affected element.

Example:

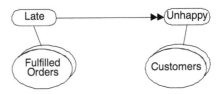

Collaborates

A line connector with *two sets of double-headed arrows* meeting in the center is used to illustrate that two or more elements are *collaborating* with one another. Generally, this implies a harmonious relationship.

Example:

In agreement with

A line connector with a *solid circle* at each end is used to illustrate that two or more elements are in *agreement*.

Example:

Equal, Same

A line connector with an *equal sign* is used to illustrate that something is *equal* or the *same* as something else. This is frequently found in the "as is" analysis, but discouraged in the "to be" proposal.

Example:

PROCESS DESCRIPTORS

Flow of Control

A *dashed line* with an *arrowhead* on the end is used to illustrate the *flow of control* between sequential steps of a process or activity.

Example:

Decision, Choice

A *multiple tree fork* on the flow of control is used to illustrate a *decision* or *choice* between different workflow alternatives. The flow of control continues along the chosen workflow process or activity.

Example:

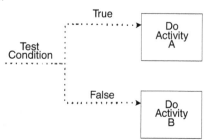

Parallel,
Concurrent

A *double set of vertical parallel lines* is used to illustrate *parallel* or *concurrent processing* within the boundary of the lines. Multiple processes or activities are initiated simultaneously and may execute concurrently. All processes or activities within the boundary must be complete before the next workflow process or activity can continue.

Example:

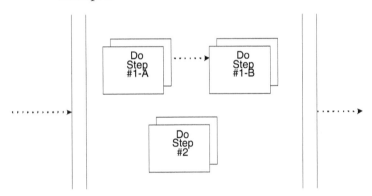

Loop Condition

An *oval* is used to illustrate a *loop condition*. The loop continues until the annotated condition is met. Loops may exist inside of other loops.

Example:

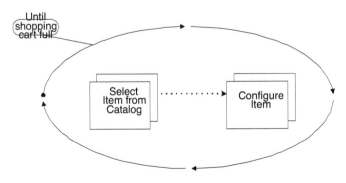

An *octagon* is used to illustrate a *wait condition*. Processing is stopped until the annotated condition is satisfied, then processing continues with the next workflow process or activity.

Example:

DESCRIPTORS

No, Not

The *international "no" symbol* is used to illustrate a *"no"* or *"not"* condition.

Example:

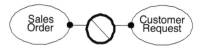

A small *horizontal box with rounded edges* is used to *describe* an element. It is used very much like an adjective or adverb. If a process under analysis is described as "too slow," then further analysis may discover opportunities for improvement.

Example:

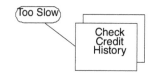

State

A small *horizontal box* is used to illustrate the *state* of a *technology input or output*. A customer in the customer technology repository (or database) may have a state of "active" or "inactive." These indicate the changes of state of a technology output.

Example:

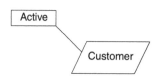

A *blocked arrow* is used to illustrate an *event*. An event initiates a process and causes it to execute.

Example:

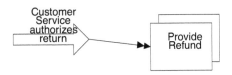

A *blocked arrow* with a darkened border is used to illustrate an *external event*.

Example:

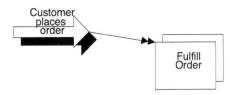

An open box with an attached line is used to record *temporary notes*, issues, or questions. Once resolved, the note is removed.

REFERENCES

1. James Martin, *The Great Transition: Using the Seven Disciplines of Enterprise Engineering to Align People, Technology, and Strategy* (New York: American Management Association, 1995), 104.

EBA–ML QUICK REFERENCE

Descriptors

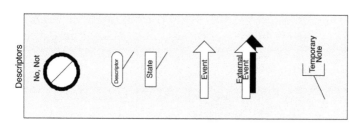

No, Not

Descriptor

State

Event

External Event

Temporary Note

Connectors

Causes

Collaborates

In agreement with

Equal, Same

=

Aggregations

Whole/Part

Shared Properties

Contains

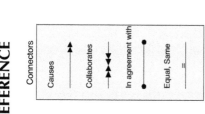

Process Descriptors

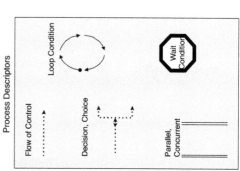

Loop Condition

Flow of Control

Decision, Choice

Parallel, Concurrent

Wait Condition

Connectors

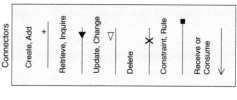

Create, Add

+

Retrieve, Inquire

Update, Change

Delete

Constraint, Rule

Receive or Consume

Entities

Enterprise or Business Unit

External Entity

Inputs and Outputs

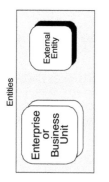

Physical I/O

Technology I/O

Aggregated Physical I/O

Aggregated Technology I/O

Business Processes and Technology Applications

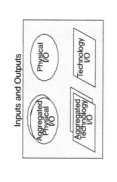

Value Stream

Lowest Level Activity

Lowest Level Application or Method

Aggregated Value Streams

Aggregated Processes

Aggregated Application or Method

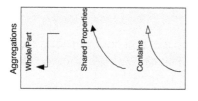
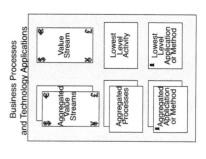

Appendix B

EBA PROJECT SCHEDULE

The following shows a representative project schedule timeline.

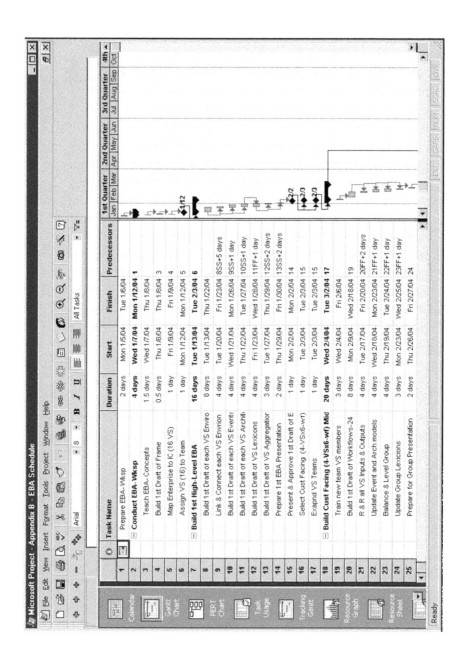

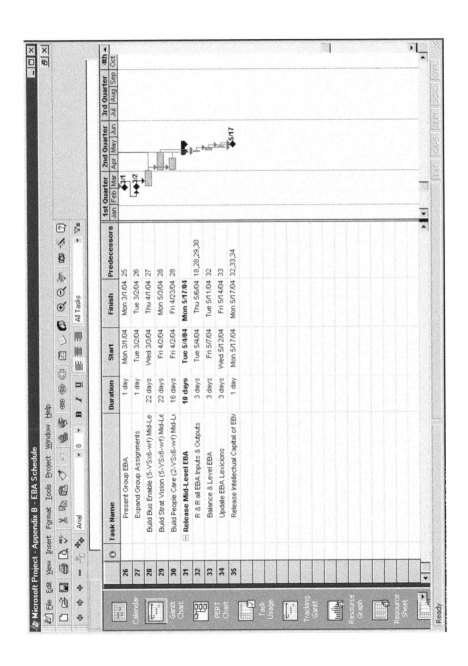

Appendix C

GLOSSARY

Aggregation b-Web: A type of b-Web that leads in a hierarchical fashion, positioning itself as a value-adding intermediary between producers and customers. For example, Wal-Mart, E*Trade.

Agora b-Web: A type of b-Web that facilitates exchange between buyers and sellers, who jointly "discover" a price through on-the-spot negotiations. For example, eBay.

Alliance b-Web: A type of b-Web that strives for high-value integration without hierarchical control. Its participants design goods or services, create knowledge, or simply produce dynamic, shared experiences. For example, Open Source, Linux.

Application Architecture: Defines the major kinds of applications needed to manage the data and support the business functions of the enterprise. It is not a design for systems, nor is it a detailed requirements analysis. It is a definition of what applications will do to manage data and provides information to people performing business functions. It also provides access to needed data in a useful format at an acceptable cost. The application architecture is defined after the data architecture is characterized. The application architecture is a catalog of applications along with the functions that they deliver and interfaces between applications. The application architecture is also mapped against the data architecture. The application is cross-referenced with one or more data items that it creates, retrieves, updates, or deletes. Application architecture links the data and business architecture to reflect applications. It supports the work activities of the business processes and provides automated procedures. Application architecture manages information storage and retrieval in support of the enterprise objectives. It addresses location considerations and how information is used.

Architecture: An architecture is defined as the structure of components, their relationships, and the principles and guidelines governing their design and evolution over time. Architectures are like blueprints, drawings, or models. Refers to an organized set of elements with clear relationships to one another, which together form a whole defined by its finality.

Balanced Model: All external inputs and outputs in a higher-level (parent) model require representation in a lower-level (child) model. The two levels of models are then defined as in balance.

Bill of Processes (BOP): Is to an enterprise as the bill of materials (BOM) is to an airplane. In a similar manner, it also allows you to understand the decomposition of the enterprise with an architectural diagram to understand how all of the parts fit together to form a whole.

Business Engineering: The convergence of business, information, and natural systems thinking into the new discipline.

Business Event: Something that happens outside an enterprise (external) or business area (internal to the enterprise), to which the enterprise must react in a preplanned way (business response). An external business event is caused by an external entity. An internal event is caused by another enterprise business process. A temporal event is caused by the passage of time. A synchronous event requires that multiple things happen before it is activated. Examples:

> *External* — Customer places order. External events may only come from a customer (or someone acting on behalf of a customer, e.g., a sales rep), vendor, partner, or other external entity.

> *Internal* — Company announces a product upgrade. Internal events may only come from a corporate enterprise business process.

> *Temporal* — Time to close the general ledger. Temporal events may only come from predefined enterprise business policies and schedules. Some temporal events are dictated by generally accepted accounting practices or governing agencies.

> *Synchronous* — In Web ordering, the completion of both determining item availability and credit checking, which then allows processing to continue.

Business events will have at least one business response (some more than one) and perhaps initiate other internal business events. The enterprise level models will only show the business event and assume the aggregation of the business response. However, the enterprise business model will represent the other initiated internal business events. Business events are written in present tense, using subject-predicate-object format.

Business Function/Process Model: Defined as a set of models illustrating the functional groupings of a business. These are further subdivided into two groups:

Primary, which directly relate to the business of the enterprise (e.g., operations)

Supporting, which enable the primary functionality (e.g., finance)

Each functional group contains several unique business processes (e.g., for finance, there are accounting and asset management). This model is useful for describing the enterprise because the functions remain generally constant. The business may change its organizational structure and its processes, but the basic functions remain relatively more stable.

Business Instance: The specific set of circumstances unique to a business event, which causes variation within the business event.

Customer places order (business event)

- Domestic Web order with a credit card (business instance)
- TeleSales domestic order using a corporate account (business instance)

Business Principles: The business rules on how the enterprise will conduct its business in the future.

Business Use Case: A business use case discusses how a business responds to a customer or an event. The business use case model describes high-level business processes and provides the context and source of information for expressing the system's use cases. In business modeling, we use the same concept of use case (as defined in UML) but at the level of the whole business rather than only the system under consideration.

Business Web: A new business form brought about by the information age: fluid congregations of businesses sometimes highly structured, sometimes amorphous, that come together on the Internet to create value for customers and wealth for their shareholders.

b-Web: *See* Business Web.

Capability: A capability is a value stream — an end-to-end set of activities that deliver results to a customer (internal or external). A strategic capability is a value stream critical to competing, performed at a level of excellence difficult for competing companies to copy.

Competitive Advantage: Delivering a product at lower cost or offering unique benefits to the buyer that justify a premium price.

Component: A nontrivial, nearly independent, and replaceable part of a system that fulfills a clear function in the context of a well-defined architecture. The component conforms to and provides the physical realization of a set of interfaces.

Component Architecture: One that ensures that all of the parts for a particular entity fit together properly. Conceptually, we need a component architecture for an enterprise, that is, one that allows all of the activities, inputs, and outputs of the enterprise to fit together by design. Note that component and architecture are two intertwined concepts: the architecture identifies components, their interfaces, and their interactions along several dimensions, and components exist only relative to a given architecture. You cannot mix and match your chosen components if they have not been made to fit.

Convergent Engineering: Business design implemented directly in software with an absolute minimum of translation or restatement.

Core Competency: A key technology or skill that can be used in many products. Once a corporation has mastered a set of core competencies, it can introduce, faster than its competition, diverse new products that employ these competencies. A core competency is something that a corporation does better than its competition, that the competition cannot emulate quickly, and that can be used in many products. For example, Honda with engines, 3M with sticky stuff, Sony with miniaturization, and Canon with precision optics. A bundle of skills and technologies that enable a company to provide a benefit to a customer. It represents the sum of learning across individual skill sets and individual organizational units. A core competency is very unlikely to reside in its entirety in a single individual or small team. It complements a strategic capability.

Customer-Centric View: One that focuses on the perception that the customer has of an enterprise. A customer rarely views the enterprise in terms of a single department, but rather as the product or service that is delivered and paid for.

Data: The atomic bits of fact that constitute the raw material of knowing about our business. That which is measurable and captured by instrument, device, or observation.

Data Architecture: Identifies and defines the major kinds of data that support the business functions defined in the business model. These definitions become the standards to be subsequently used for logical database design, physical database design, and database creation. It usually consists of the entity relationship diagrams, logical tables, and supporting documentation.

Decomposition: The art and science of the separation of an entity into constituent parts or elements or into simpler compounds in such a manner as to allow reconstruction back into the original entity or whole.

Diagrams: Diagrams are just pictures that require interpretation by the viewer.

Distributive Networks b-Web: A type of b-Web that services the other types of b-Webs by allocating and delivering goods, whether information, objects, money, or resources, from providers to users. For example, AT&T.

Enterprise Architecture Planning (EAP): Enterprise architecture planning is the process of defining architectures for the use of information in support of the business and the plan for implementing those architectures. There are three architectures: data, applications, and technology. EAP is a process for defining the top two layers of the Zachman Information Systems Framework.

Enterprise Business Architecture (EBA): Defines the enterprise value streams and their relationships to all external entities and other enterprise value streams and the events that trigger instantiation. The EBA serves as the central plexus of the enterprise. It is a definition of what the enterprise must produce to satisfy its customers, compete in a market, deal with its suppliers, sustain operations, and care for its employees. It is composed of architectures, workflows, and events.

Enterprise Business Process: A specific ordering of work activities across time and place, with a beginning, an end, and clearly defined inputs and outputs. A structure for action defining how work is done. Enterprise business processes are the structures by which organizations physically do what is necessary to produce value for its customers. Types:

Real value added — Order-to-Cash

Business value added — Requisition-to-Payables

Event: *See also* Business Event. Something that happens and requires some processing. Examples of events are instructions given by managers, decisions to start or end an action, failure of a machine, or signal exceeding a fixed threshold.

Framework: A collection of elements put together for some purpose. We can refer to a framework for enterprise modeling as defining the scope, concepts, and methods necessary for modeling an enterprise.

Functional Thinker: An individual who describes the business of an enterprise in terms of what it does, and the organizations or departments that perform the various activities.

Functions: A set of specialized activities with similar behaviors. Any of a group of related actions contributing to a larger action. A group of business disciplines, processes, and procedures, which together support a major aspect of an enterprise. Credit checking, applying payments, and dunning overdue accounts are functions of receivables. Receivables, payables, budgeting, and closing the corporate books are functions of accounting.

Information: Data in some recognizable form that shows us one or more patterns that may justify a change in our enterprise. The direction or resource allocation of an enterprise can be determined from the patterns found in information. The synthesis of data into patterns, trends, or behaviors.

Information Architecture: Consists of data models and databases that serve all participants in the business and its strategies, standards, and policies. The information architecture requires that the enterprise stop developing isolated or independent databases and design a common, up-to-date, shared, distributed, and consistent data repository. Establishes the decision-making principles and standards for the use of information as a business resource. It facilitates the establishment of the underlying infrastructure for managing the information asset.

Initiative: The classification and grouping of opportunities that focus and contribute to the same business objective, value stream, product/service offering, or common problems.

Insight: The highest level of abstraction relating to data, information, and knowledge. Having insight means understanding the meaning of knowledge, seeing the implications of decisions far in advance. It also takes on the dimension of morality or ethical behavior because larger cultural implications are related to the factual; insight can address the questions of good and bad. It is reflected as much in the questions asked as in the resulting data analysis; these questions elicit analyses that are less "how" than "why." These questions seek to turn up the unexpected, the far-out, and the unseen.

Integrated Enterprise Architecture: The style and method of design and construction that comprise the elements of a system and define the purposes and interrelationships of those elements.

Integration b-Web: *See* Value Chain b-Web.

IT Principles: The technology rules on how IT will enable support and conduct business.

Knowledge: Information taken to the next level of abstraction, relating to data and information, which is revealed in relationships. The ability to extrapolate, to make decisions on information that is not yet reality, is found in knowledge. The synthesis of information into predictable results.

Market Maker b-Web: *See* Agora b-Web.

Methodology: Refers to a set of methods, models, and tools to be used in a structured way to solve a problem.

Mission: Concise, high-level statement of an enterprise's basic purpose or reason for existence.

Model: A model is a useful representation of some subject. It is an abstraction of a reality expressed in terms of some language defined by modeling constructs for the purpose of the user. A model is always expressed in terms of a language. This language is more or less formatted and is made of constructs. A model is simplification of reality that completely describes a system from a particular perspective. We build models of complex systems because we cannot otherwise comprehend such systems in their entirety. Models have semantic interpretations that are consistent and inherently understood.

Modeling Construct: A modeling construct is a primitive of a modeling language, the syntax and semantics of which must be precisely defined. Formal description techniques are defined by constructs having a good syntax and semantics.

Modeling Tool: Modeling tools are based on a repository that allows the objects to be reused in contexts other than the specific diagram where they originated. A repository can assist in verifying the results of models, transform models into another format, and reuse the objects and components of some models to build other models. In contrast, business diagramming tools have no semantic understanding of the diagram that has been built. The ability to reuse, extend, and transform a diagram into another format is nonexistent and can only occur via manual translation and integration by an analyst.

Network/Technology Architecture: *See* Technology Architecture.

Objective: Broad, quantifiable outcome statements describing what the enterprise would like to accomplish to achieve its vision.

Opportunity: A clearly defined solution to an identified gap between the "as is" and "to be" states.

Organizational Architecture: This architecture consists of three aspects of corporate organization: (1) the assignment of decision rights within the company, (2) the methods of rewarding individuals, and (3) the systems to evaluate the performance of both individuals and business units. Deals with the structure for providing products and services and the management of those products and services. Deals with the business and organizational management of providing business and IT services and products, the management of the services, IT systems and network management (to include security), and element management. It includes policies, governance, functions, skills, roles, and responsibilities.

Process Thinker: An individual who describes the business of an enterprise in terms of what it produces in relationship to its customers, suppliers, competitors, cross-functional processes, and organizational activities.

Rational Unified Process (RUP): A software engineering process. It provides a disciplined approach to assigning tasks and responsibilities within a development organization. Its goal is to ensure the production of high-quality software that meets the needs of its end users within a predictable schedule and budget.

Schema: A structured framework that is a codification of rules, constructs, icons, and experience that adheres to a rigorous set of disciplines built around a particular set of semantics and syntax.

Security Architecture: A security architecture describes the services, mechanisms, and components that reflect the security policy, business functions, and technology of an enterprise. The whole notion of protection involves three areas: security, continuity, and control. The primary purpose of a security architecture is to ensure a common level of understanding and a common basis for design and implementation by everyone sharing the same resources.

Strategic Business Planning: Strategic business planning is the process of defining the vision and long-term objectives for the business and the strategies for achieving them. It is a process that requires frequent updates based on the changing nature of the markets served.

Strategic Capability: A strategic capability is a value stream critical to competing, performed at a level of excellence difficult for competing companies to copy. It complements a core competency.

Strategic IT Planning: Strategic IT planning is the process of defining frameworks and architectures in support of the business and creating the plan for implementing those frameworks and architectures. It is a process that requires frequent updates based on the changing nature of the business strategy.

Supply Chain: The set of inter- and intracompany processes that produce and deliver goods and services to customers. It includes activities such as material sourcing, production scheduling, and the physical distribution system, backed up by the necessary information flows. Procurement, manufacturing, inventory management, warehousing, and transportation are typically considered part of the supply chain organization. Product development, demand forecasting, order entry, channel management, customer service, and accounts payable and receivable lie in a gray area; in theory, they are part of the supply chain process, but they are seldom included within the supply chain organization. Marketing, sales, finance, and strategic planning are not. This cycle of buy-make-move-store-sell is called the supply chain.

SWOT: Strengths, weaknesses, opportunities, and threats.

System Use Case: A system use case is an interaction with the software.

Technology Architecture: Defines the major kinds of technologies needed to provide an environment for the applications that are managing data. It is not a detailed requirements analysis or a design of enterprise computing networks and software. Rather, it defines the kinds of technologies referred to as platforms that will support the business with a shared data environment. Technology platforms are the pipeline and physical facilities of a data utility. The technology architecture is a depiction of all technology components. A technology architecture is built by breaking down a system into component technology items such as server computer, user workstation, graphical user interface, RDBMS (relational database management system), and data dictionary/repository, and then selecting candidates based on evaluation criteria such as compliance to ANSI (American National Standards Institute) and industry standards, cost, and compliance with internal standards. This is what links up with the application, business, and information architectures to provide interoperable technology platforms that meet the needs of the various user roles at identified work locations. Should be defined after the data and applications architectures to ensure that the technology platforms are reasonable, feasible, and consistent with the other architectures.

Test Scenario: A description of a real-world situation that occurs in the enterprise. Based on a particular set of circumstances, it will cause or invoke various activities, directly or indirectly, to occur and create identifiable results, outcomes, or outputs for validation.

Unified Modeling Language (UML): UML is the industry standard language for specifying, visualizing, constructing, and documenting the artifacts of software systems. It simplifies the complex process of software design, making a blueprint for construction. The effort defining the UML was led by Rational Software's industry-leading methodologists: Grady Booch, Ivar Jacobson, and Jim Rumbaugh.

Use Case: A use case is a sequence of actions a system performs that yields an observable result or value to a particular actor.

Value Chain: The disaggregating of a firm into its strategically relevant activities to understand the behavior of costs and the existing and potential sources of differentiation.

Value Chain b-Web: A type of b-Web where the context provider structures and directs a b-Web network to produce a highly integrated value proposition. The output meets a customer order or market opportunity. The seller has the final say in pricing. For example, Cisco.

Value Nets: This introduces an entirely new class of business designs — designs that deliver new and unique levels of service and personalized products to customers. Value nets integrate the essential front-end understanding of customer needs with the crucial back end that precisely delivers on the front-end promise. Value nets are digital, collaborative, agile powerhouses that unlock hidden profits for shareholders. They begin by capturing what is important to different customers and work back to physical production and distribution processes enabled by unifying information flow design. A business design that uses digital supply chain concepts to achieve both superior customer satisfaction and company profitability.

Value Proposition: For the market space in question, what value is offered, delivered, and consumed that justifies a business's right to exist. A value proposition is a statement of how value is to be delivered to customers. It is important both internally and externally. Internally, it identifies the value drivers it is attempting to offer to a target customer group and the activities involved in producing the value together with the cost drivers involved in the value-producing activities. Externally, it is the means by which a firm positions the enterprise in the minds of customers.

Value Stream: An end-to-end collection of activities that create a result for a customer, who may be the ultimate customer or an internal end user of the value stream. The value stream has a clear goal: to satisfy or to delight the customer. Value streams differ from functions in that a value stream is a cycle of activity that begins with a specified event and ends when a specified output is produced.

Vision: Energizing, positive, and inspiring statement of what the future enterprise looks like at the end of the planning period.

Workflow: Graphically portrays how inputs are transformed to outputs for the enterprise. Workflows illustrate the flow of control, delays, sequencing, and which entity performs the activity. Workflows are dynamic models that require activation by an event.

Appendix D

ENTERPRISE BUSINESS ARCHITECTURE WEB SITE

The linking and integration capabilities of an Enterprise Business Architecture are hard to illustrate using the typical format of a book page. The smaller pages make the models somewhat difficult to read and understand. Therefore, we built a Web site for viewing and navigating through the models in html format. A vertical section of the Enterprise Hierarchy, focusing on the Order-to-Cash value stream, is provided on the Web site for review by interested readers. The example provided is the same one depicted in Figure 6.1.

Please refer to our Web site at:

http://www.enterprisebusinessarchitecture.com.

Click on **Case Study Models** to navigate through the EBA example.

INDEX

INDEX

H

I

Milton Keynes UK
Ingram Content Group UK Ltd.
UKHW031130141024
449569UK00006B/290